Legendary London

and the Spirit of Place

New Light on the Great Changes of our Times

Legendary London

and the Spirit of Place

New Light on the Great Changes of our Times

Edited by
Anthony Thorley

Illustrations by
Peter Dawkins, Chris Street,
Anthony Thorley and **Ian Thorp**

ARCHIVE publishing

First published in Great Britain by
Archive Publishing
Wimborne, Dorset, England

Designed at Archive Publishing by Ian Thorp
for the Gatekeeper Trust

A CIP Record for this book is available from
the British Cataloguing in Publication data office.

ISBN 978-1-906289-22-5 (paperback)

Cover painting of the Thames by Moonlight by Henry Pether circa 1828-1862

www.transpersonalbooks.com

Printed and bound in Malta
by Melita Press

CONTENTS

The ArcelorMittal Orbit sculpture in the London Olympic Park is designed to be a permanent and enduring symbol of the London 2012 Games. Challenging and controversial, can it achieve legendary status like the London Eye or the Eiffel Tower in Paris?

INTRODUCTION

In the summer of 2012 London hosts the Olympic and Paralympic Games. For the third time in modern Olympic history, athletes and spectators from all nations come to Britain to take part in the greatest festival of sport on our planet. This is truly a meeting of the global family where, in the tradition of the Olympic truce of the ancient Games in Greece, wars and disputes, oppressions and inequalities are all put aside, national athletic teams seek to enact through the Olympic ideal pride and success through free and open competition on an even playing field. It iswidely acknowledged that the Olympic spirit is unique to the Olympic Games. While sought after in other international athletic and sporting meetings, nowhere is it more certain that whilst athletes and their support teams face each other in fierce competition and pride in their individual nations, they are also united in the brotherhood and sisterhood of the Olympic spirit. For many athletes and their support staff, the Olympic Festival of 2012 is the peak experience of their sporting careers and lifelong athletic endeavours. For many spectators, the spectacle of the Games could be literally the time of their lives. For London, this is the culmination of an Olympic Dream.

The Games carry such a rich tradition of ancient myth and legend and a history of so many past and present heroes that it is impossible for a host country not to be drawn into profound participation in this mythic stream and its potential for cultural transformation. This was of course present in tensions during the run-up to the initial Olympic bid to host the games, the necessary deep levels of financial and cultural commitment, the wholehearted support of government and the administration of the host city, and finally the will of the people of that city to welcome the world athletic family, recognising that through this sporting event their city will be touched by history, never to be quite the same again. Whatever the impact of the Games and future Olympic heritage might turn out to be, it is undeniable that no one, however materially commercial, enthusiastically patriotic, romantically spiritual or determinedly disinterested can entirely escape this opportunity for profound transformation.

It is also apparent, however, that the specific and more local promise of transformation of the Games in London is significantly matched by the deeper streams of transformative energy which beset us all at a wider level in these early years of the twenty-first century. All over the world the basic principles of our individual and national existence are being challenged as never before. We are discovering how fragile our interdependence is and that there is no real possibility of national, political, financial and perhaps most of all environmental isolation. We cannot escape global warming, financial meltdown and issues of national and military security. The failures of doctrinal communism are matched by the dubious success of capitalism. We see there are many challenges to realise true democracy and are aware of the embarrassingly poor examples of effective western government that can be held up as inspiration to those parts of the world struggling to break the shackles of institutional dictatorship and family oligarchy. These are the problems that we read about and see on our TV screens every day of our lives. Unavoidably interdependent members of a global family, we are living in times of great change.

The Value of Myth and Legend

It is against this background that the authors of this book have come together to present a unique perspective on the spirit of London and the profound times of change in which we live. The book reflects the premise that behind the relative certainty in accounts of our national history lies a legendary vein of stories and traditions that contain a rich stream of national myth which deeply affects our everyday life today. While it might be conventional to judge history as valuable for at least having some basis in fact and relevant interpretation, legend, whilst interesting in its own right, is seen as less relevant because it is founded more in the imagination and cannot be certainly true. Myth, the deepest level of our national story, is generally be held to be of the wildest fantasy and totally fictional, and therefore of minimal significance to contemporary life.

The authors dispute this conventional view. Whilst acknowledging that objective history is absolutely essential for us to understand our past, construct our present and best avoid pitfalls in the future, we also value the role played out in our ordinary lives by legend and myth. Legends and the deeper levels of myth may be barely testable against historical facts, or when they are, usually fail dismally, but they do carry a deeper and fundamental truth which is often integrated into our most elemental beliefs and ideas. It might be said that myth is the living undercurrent of our culture, the journey of our folk-soul richly enacted through legend and powerfully supported by unfolding history. And the sources of our myth are to be found in the deepest origins of the people we are: the ancient Britons and the cosmopolitan family of nations that make up modern London. When we look to stories of our origins or the origins of our cities, we look to the rivers that flow through them and the character of the landscape and countryside around them.

So the sources of inspiration for the chapters that follow are less about historical characters than legendary enactments of ancient gods, goddesses and mythic beings that have been strongly identified with sacred waters, fertile plains, high places and mountains. It goes without saying that all peoples seek a founding story for their origins and the origins of their capital city, the British no less than any other, and the example of the tale of Brutus or Brit the Trojan warrior and the London Stone amply fills this mythic need.

Brutus and the London Stone

Like many other cities of Europe, London claims its origins in the after-math of the Trojan War, that great turning point and doorway into western classical civilisation in the distant Bronze Age of the eastern Mediterranean. Who can blame cities seeking the imprimatur of such a refined classical civilisation for their own? Ulysses in his wanderings founded Lisbon in Portugal, Aeneas led his party from Troy to found Rome and Brutus, his grandson, with his own party of Trojan adventurers made land at Totnes, in England's West Country. Previously, and before any

Brutus of Troy

The Brutus Stone in Totnes, Devon

existence of London, Britain had been ruled by a race of giants, led by Albion, whose name became adopted as Britain's own. Albion's successor giants were Gogmagog and his companions, and after a telling battle against these great beings, Brutus' champion Corineus faced Gogmagog in single combat. Eventually, Corineus overcame Gogmagog and threw him over a cliff which still bears the giant's name. The fight secured the region known today as Cornwall (so named after Corineus), and Brutus commemorated his success by setting up the Brutus Stone in Totnes, where (and this is how myth becomes real) it can still be seen today.

Brutus and his Trojan friends then made their way across southern Britain to the plains of the river Thames where they found a people called Trinovanti. Recognising distant Trojan relatives, Brutus founded a city on the banks of the Thames and called it Caer Troia, Troy Town or Trinovantium. This would be the future city of King Lud which eventually would be called London. But again, Brutus set his mark on his new city not only by giving his own name (Brut or Brit) to the conquered Britons but also by setting up another Brutus Stone, more commonly called the London Stone. This Stone carries extraordinary symbolic and indeed real qualities and as we shall see, its mythical status is strengthened by passing history.

It is claimed that the Stone came from an old stone circle on Ludgate Hill and that Brutus used it for part of an altar dedicated to the goddess Diana. It first appears historically in the early tenth century and was established as a large column standing in Candlewick Street (now Cannon Street) in the twelfth century.

The myth then arose that the safety of the Stone was linked to the security of London itself, remembered in the saying: 'So long as the Stone of Brutus is safe, so long shall London flourish'. All distances measured out of London radiate from this revered Stone, which took on the status of an omphalos representing the navel of the world. Incorporated into the title of the first mayors of London, the Stone became the site of all important oath-taking and key announcements. In 1450 the rebel Jack Cade, entering London with his forces, struck the Stone with his sword and declared himself 'Lord of the City', an event dramatised in Shakespeare's *Henry VI, Part 2*. By the seventeenth century the Stone was smaller, possibly damaged by passing wagons, and could be found outside St Swithin's Church on the north side of Cannon Street. The thirteenth-century church (always named St Swithin's London Stone) was due to be rebuilt after the Fire of London in 1666 and it seems that Christopher Wren may have intended to incorporate the Stone into a grand piazza as part of his new plan for the city. Even though this ambitious scheme never came to fruition, Wren held the Stone important enough to have it protected with a stone covering near the wall of the rebuilt church.

A nineteenth-century engraving showing the London Stone in the wall of St Swithin's Church

Wren considered the Stone most likely to originally have been part of a Roman house, whilst others speculated that it might have been a Roman milestone. By 1798 it was moved again, and by 1828, possibly even smaller in size, it was set into a niche in the wall of St Swithin's. Miraculously surviving the destruction of the church in World War II bombing during 1940, there it remained until 1962, when it was moved into a backlit, grilled niche in the new Bank of China building. Barely visible to the passing bystander, it still stands there today. This building is part of a major re-development in the Cannon Street area and around 2008, the Stone was close to being removed as just another piece of rubble. Fortunately, attention of its status as an iconic representation of the survival of London was drawn to the Museum of London, which pledged to ensure its future safety and probable relocation into a new office development. Such is the passing mythology, legendary status and genuine history, both ancient and modern, of the London Stone. Too small now for us to ever know the exact nature of its origin, whether milestone, altar-stone or standing-stone, the Stone, identified as Clipsham Oolite Limestone, is known to have come from a quarry in Rutland, some hundred miles north of London and well-known for its use in Roman times.

Outline of the Book

Carrying such a tradition of continuity from earliest origins, through fires, wars, damage and bombing to current City of London redevelopment, it is not surprising that the legendary London Stone is referenced at least three times in the contributions which make up this book. Not only does the

Stone satisfy all the criteria of active myth, legend and history, it also fulfils all the conditions to be considered sacred, and the place of its current repose, however apparently insignificant, carries all the features of a sacred site. This apparent paradox serves to remind us that London is above all a sacred city, not only because of its numerous churches and places of worship but also because many of its key features and places, great and small, well-known and more secret, carry that quality of the numinous, where ordinary time and space seem momentarily suspended and an individual may experience some significant alteration of consciousness, or at least a profound sense of wonder or awe.

All the authors' contributions emphasise the powerful effect of sacred place, whether it is the springs at the origin of a great river, the landscape contributing to a chakric system, or a pattern of energies which cohere into the effigies of a zodiac or living temple. Myth in the landscape is both archaic and contemporary, and is always re-inventing itself in the context of the predominant cultural issues of the day. Seventy years ago that would have been the context of a World War and the survival of a city under threat. Today, the myth can be seen as expressed in the synchronicities and wonder generated by the presence of the Olympic Games and the occasion of the Diamond Jubilee. Goddesses like Isis and gods such as Lugh, representing streams of focussed consciousness barely considered for centuries, suddenly thrust themselves into the fore in the energy of the current mythic undercurrent and are seen to play a profound role in contemporary events and the realisation of the Olympic Dream.

Louise Coe unfolds the contribution made to London's history by its two main rivers, the Thames and the Lea. The Thames, a combination of Thame and Isis, draws water from the whole of south England and around it has developed one of the great cities of the world, a beacon of national security and a great trading centre which still focuses its international contribution on commerce and finance. The Lea, the river of Lugh, where the games are sited, expresses the energy of invention and novel thinking, the powerhouse of London's commercial production and working class culture. Coe shows how these two energies combine in the lower Lea Valley to reflect their traditional gods and goddesses and provide the impetus for the current Olympic vision.

Peter Dawkins examines the claim that, above all, London was anciently founded as a dragon city, incorporating a winding chakric system of energy points that originate at the Root near the Tower of London and culminate in the Brow and Crown energies at the top of Ludgate Hill. Here now stand the Stock Exchange of Brow-like knowledge and St Paul's Cathedral reflecting the expression of the highest Crown-like spiritual aspiration. As modern myth continues to act itself out in this powerful living dragon landscape, it is no surprise that the 2011 Occupy anti-capitalism protest tent encampment occupied the exact interface of these two chakric energies by St Paul's Cathedral and has produced such fundamental challenges for both the commercial and the ecclesiastical establishments.

Chris Street takes us through the pattern of energies that appear to literally guard London as a sacred city. Etched into the street pattern and the rivers around the periphery of the city are a giant Lion and Unicorn, potent echoes of the heraldic beasts supporting our national coat of arms. The Lion incorporates part of the Lea Valley and brings additional symbolic or mythic energy to the Olympic site.

Using the example of the original Shakespearean Globe Theatre, Peter Dawkins explores how its architecture and symbolism were based on ancient esoteric science and mythology, enabling drama that can purify the emotions and so be a mouthpiece and major influence on London's deeper consciousness and creative culture, a process exemplified by the myth of the Swan. This myth generates a profound connection which goes far beyond London and has energetic and cultural dimensions which reach out and affect the entire world.

Anthony Thorley shows how after the Great Fire of London in 1666, Christopher Wren and others tried to convince the King, Parliament and the City of London that a great new city plan based on pure number and geometric balance should be pursued in order to place London at the fore-front of great European cities. The plan was rejected for practical reasons but in his subsequent rebuilding of city churches, Wren appears to have enshrined for posterity the main imprint of his city plan with all its protective advantages of survival and triumph through adversity.

Thorley also presents the story of the great pre-Roman pan-European god Lugh and his association with the ancient great festival in August of the beginning of the harvest, Lughnasa. He explores the way Lugh's presence in the British landscape culminates in the source of the River Lea, or Lugh, at Luton to flow down and embrace the Olympic site at Stratford, so creating a global Lughnasa. Through the examples of landscape zodiacs and their remarkable properties of concentrated synchronicity, Thorley explains the tradition of the Gypsy Switch Zodiac that lies round Britain and how the Galactic Centre of that great zodiacal system is situated exactly on the site of the Olympic Park.

In a short afterword, the book discusses the wider implications of these mythic and legendary themes and the part they play in the great worldwide changes that affect us all at this time.

The main thrust and stimulus for these contributions comes from a series of annual conferences and pilgrimage walks organised and funded by the Gatekeeper Trust on the theme 'The Enchantment of Olympic

The London Stone as seen today behind its iron grill

London' which commenced in 2008 and culminated in the Olympic year of 2012. These conferences and walks have explored a much broader and more complex canvas that is beyond the scope of this book but we are grateful to have been able to present some of the key features for a wider audience. Details of the work of the Gatekeeper Trust are provided at the end of the book.

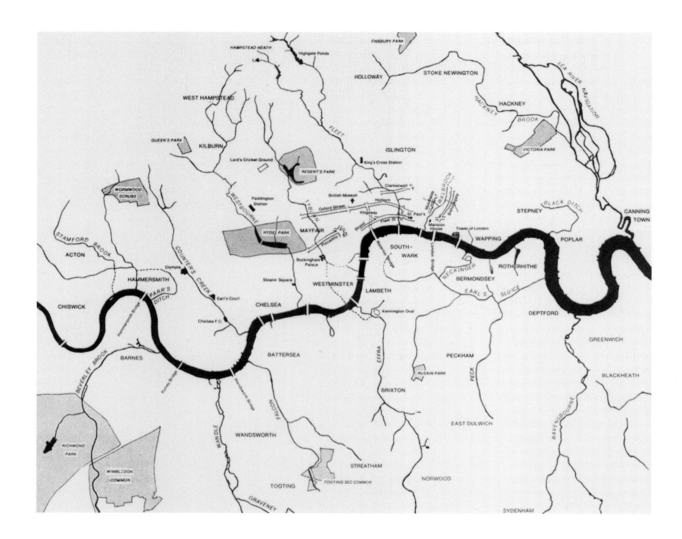

*The lost Rivers
of London*

LIQUID HISTORY:
THE SACRED WATERS OF LONDON

Louise Coe

London is a city of rivers. Visitors know that they have truly arrived in the heart of London when they find themselves gazing down on the Thames from one of the many bridges that now span the river, which threads its way like a deep dark grey-blue ribbon through the buildings that flank it river on either side. We tend to forget that London is the river's city, growing up along the banks of the Thames, formed and shaped by its meandering course.

The Thames is not London's only river, however. Central London is located on an alluvial flood plain formed by the meandering Thames and fed by its tributary streams. Some dozen or more of these tributaries flow from the surrounding high hills: to the north at Neasden, Hampstead and Hornsey and to the south at Streatham, Dulwich and Forest Hill. Since for the most part they now lie buried deep underground, the many rivers flowing down to the Thames are known as the lost rivers of London. But these lost rivers still have their influence and if you know where to look, you can find their traces all across London.

Every river, stream and spring has its own particular energy and character, incorporating mythical, legendary and historical associations that contribute to creating the spirit of place. The sweeping curves and meanders of the Thames through London bring a unique spirited flourish, matched by powerful and complex fast flowing tidal waters. This is a river that commands respect.

London's second river is the Lea, which meets the Thames as it widens and creates one of its most dramatic arching curves before leaving the city behind and making its way firmly out to sea. It is a further sixty miles to the open sea but it is from this point onwards that the tidal waters become much stronger. Today, the influence of the sea upon London is no longer so evident and we can easily forget that this is a port city.

A City of Trade

Perceiving the economic advantages of the river, the Romans founded their city of Londinium on the north bank at the point where the Walbrook River meets the Thames. The tide sweeps in twice a day and the Romans appreciated the fact that their ships could be borne upstream from the sea by the force of the water alone. Since the river is tidal in both directions, ships that were carried on the incoming tide could just as well benefit from the ebb tide to carry them downriver back out to sea. The Romans also understood the value of London's strategic position on the Thames, offering a gateway into the country and also a gateway to the Rhine and their trading partners overseas. From the outset, Londinium was more a trading centre than a military base and it is merchandise and financial skills which have driven the city ever since.

London's wealth was built on sea-faring trade and has prospered greatly over the years, beyond what could have been expected. Twelfth-century London was already an ancient port, vividly described in the 1180s by the clerk William Fitzstephen, who wrote of the merchants bringing in 'Arabia's gold, Sabae's spice and incense, Scythia's keen weapons, and the oil of palms from Babylon's rich soil, Nile's precious gems, Norway's

A model of the north bank of Roman London c. 90 CE, showing part of the first bridge across the Thames

warm peltries, Russia's costly sables, Sera's rich vestures and the wines of Gaul'.

London was for centuries a thriving centre for trade, with the Thames at the centre of possibility. By the sixteenth century this was the largest city in the world. As well as transporting cargo, the river was the main highway for Londoners who would jump on a boat to travel from one place to the next, as we today hop on a bus or catch a taxi. So many ships and boats jostling on the water often caused traffic jams and it became dangerous to navigate, while the noise by day and night drowned out any sound of the river's flow.

This chaotic bustling waterway, source of London's wealth, was a lawless place. Much of the trade was plundered before reaching its destination. In 1802, the first of the Docklands was built to protect the trade ships from theft and ensure full payment of tax on the cargo.

The West India Dock was the first protected commercial dock. The East India Dock and St Katherine's Dock followed and then countless others. They were constructed on a massive scale: towering vast walled expanses beyond anything seen before. Verlaine wrote 'the docks are impossible to describe. They are unbelievable, Tyre and Carthage rolled into one'. Joseph Conrad described how the 'lightless walls seemed to spring from

West India Docks in 1802 by W Daniell

the very mud upon which the stranded barges lie'. The Docklands thrived until containerised lorries made their use redundant. The age of the bustling Docklands lasted for one hundred and fifty years and then fell silent.

From the 1960s, for twenty years the area lay dormant until fresh enterprise swept in to build a new financial hub. Canary Wharf aimed to create a business district large enough to challenge the dominance of the old City of London. Ultimately the plan succeeded after some false starts and quite a few billion pounds, much of it taxpayers' money. The style is American, ownership is often American, so creating a little bit of Manhattan in London, and may owe some of its success to new business practice. The old ramshackle city buildings are not set up for the internet age whereas the Canary Wharf district is a paradise for wireless efficiencies. Many consider the hideous buildings show no regard for architectural style or spirit of place, but simply function.

Iain Sinclair, local London writer, pungently sums it up: 'A centre that could be anywhere and nowhere. The definitive repudiation of the discredited philosophy of place ... Canary Wharf had the vulgarity to climb off the drawing-board. It's Lights Out for the territory'.

With the development of the Docklands, the focus of growth shifted

Canary Wharf at night viewed from Shadwell

towards east London. Eighteenth- and nineteenth-century London saw rapid growth, with the expansion and strengthening of the British Empire, the burgeoning Industrial Revolution and a massive growth of population. It is during this period that the city expanded east to the lower Lea Valley and beyond. Historically, people have looked from London Bridge and St Paul's Cathedral westward to the great palaces and houses along the Thames: the parks, theatres and finery of a grand city. To the east, London is guarded by the Tower, beyond which the infrastructure has developed to support such refinements and enable an industrialised modern London to prosper. Even if we simply look at the story of the Thames and the Lea, we can get a sense of the different energies and personalities of these two rivers and how they have uniquely contributed to the folk-soul of London as a great city.

London's Forgotten Rivers

Before a more detailed consideration of the Thames as London's sacred river, it is worth briefly exploring three of its many tributaries to see how their different energies influence place.

The largest of London's forgotten rivers, the River Fleet has always been revered as London's sacred river, as it is said to fall 'from a higher grace than any of her sister streams'. Londoners flocked to various spas, springs and wells upstream to take the chalybeate waters, which were held to have healing properties. The Fleet actually came to be named the River of Wells because of the many wells offering healing water along its course. Further downstream, from as early as the thirteenth century, the Fleet became increasingly polluted until in the sixteenth century, Ben Jonson described how the Fleet 'outdid the four rivers of Hades in its vile stench'. Its subsequent history has been pithily described in the following terms: 'The Fleet, which started as a river, declined to a brook, dwindled to a ditch and was finally demoted to a drain'.

The Great Fire of London in 1666 provided the opportunity for rebuilding, allowing new designs and new ideas, and the architect Sir Christopher Wren converted the lower reach of the Fleet into a 'New

Canal' as elaborate as the Grand Canal in Venice. The mouth of the river was broadened and cut deeper, given stone embankments and traversed by four new decorative bridges at Bridewell, Fleet Street, Fleet Lane and Holborn. Unfortunately this plan did not succeed commercially and the Fleet was entirely covered over some twenty years later.

The Fleet rises from two springs on Hampstead Heath. After flowing through the ponds on the Heath, the stream today disappears underground and the healing waters stay underground for the rest of its five-mile course.

The origins of the Tyburn rise from Shepherd's Well in Hampstead and a second source flows from a spring on Haverstock Hill. Before this river went completely underground, channelled into conduits, the Tyburn flowed south through Swiss Cottage down to Regent's Park. At what is now St. James's Park, it split into three branches, two of which formed Thorney Island upon which Westminster Abbey was built. One branch flows through Mayfair and under Buckingham Palace before it flows into the Thames. The Tyburn has associations with Tiw, the god of justice and law, of keeping one's word and the courage to be true. It is said that there was a Druid tree college on Thorney Island, a predecessor of the current law-makers who now sit in the Houses of Parliament.

The City, the heart of London, has its own river, the Walbrook. It rises as a series of rivulets in Islington and Hoxton which merge into one stream just north of the old Roman wall and run through the city and underneath the Bank of England, entering the Thames just by Cannon Street station. As it meanders past Wren's church, St Stephen Walbrook, a sensitive

The mouth of the Fleet c. 1750 by Samuel Scott

person can feel the cold freshness of the waters while walking in the street. As we have seen, flowing waterways are key to the energy and spirit of place. So the Walbrook is an extremely significant body of water, generating commerce and financial power. However modest a waterway it may be now, this is the river that serves the Square Mile.

There is still a City of London Ward called Walbrook

Sources of the Thames

From the high ground in the west of the country, the Thames crosses England until reaching the North Sea some sixty miles east of London. Traversing a distance of two hundred and fourteen miles from source to sea, this is not a mighty river by world standards but nevertheless is the longest river in England's countryside.

As do all great rivers, the Thames rises in many places but principally at four headstreams: the Thames or Isis, the Churn, the Coln and the Leach. Of these, the two most significant sources are at Thames Head and Seven Springs.

We can see from old paintings that Thames Head was once a dramatic source, the nascent Thames gushing up from a deep well like a fountain. Nowadays, however, a walk to the marker stone in meadowland that marks the source can be disappointing. The water level has dropped and for most of the year the infant stream flows underground to rise further down-stream. Thames Head is considered to be the official source of the Thames, and is so recognised by Thames Water and various other water authorities along its length. It is preferable to walk south from Thames Head to Lyd Well, which is found in a small walled enclosure where the spring can be seen bubbling along.

Others hold the true source to be at Seven Springs near Cheltenham, a further fourteen river miles north, where a Latin inscription on the marker stone reads, 'Here O Father Thames is your Seven-fold spring'. Stone steps lead down to a pool of water into which the water flows. Source of the River Churn, Seven Springs is the highest of the tributary streams and thus considered by many to be the true source of the Thames.

Another less well-known source of the Thames' main southern

tributary, the River Kennet, is the Swallowhead Spring, nestling under the brow of Silbury Hill near the great four-thousand-year old Avebury stone circle in Wiltshire. This sacred source bursts into life each year in early springtime from a cleft in the chalky rock. The ancient Swallowhead carries a special quality of the feminine and to this day the overhanging trees are dressed with colourful ribbons, as if honouring and celebrating the emerging waters that will eventually join the Thames near Reading and then reach down into London.

It is always significant to consider first beginnings when we want to get to know a river, so it is well worth a trip to all these locations to see where the Thames emerges into the world.

As well as exploring the physical sources of a river, it is fascinating to look at how a river comes by its name. The first part of the word Thames is derived from Tamesa, a Celtic word meaning darkness or dark one. Many British rivers have this root word in their name, where the river flows dark and deep. Additionally, Tamesis is the Celtic goddess of rivers, so the Thames is honoured above all with the name of the goddess. The Celts revered the Thames as sacred and honoured the river goddess with votive offerings cast into the water, the most distinctive of which is the

The source of the Thames at Kemble

decorative bronze and enamel small shield offering which was found in the Thames at Battersea.

Confusingly, the upper reaches of the Thames have a different name. From its source until reaching Dorchester-on-Thames, quite a considerable distance downriver, the river is familiarly known as the Isis. At Dorchester, the River Isis joins the River Thame and becomes the Thame-Isis – 'dark Isis' – or Thames. As the river passes through Oxford, the Isis connection is particularly strong. Further downriver at Henley, the bridge has two keystones carved by the sculptor Anne Seymour Damer in 1785 which show Isis looking upstream and Tamesis looking downstream.

Isis is the Queen of Heaven, the all-powerful Egyptian goddess who was worshipped as the divine form of the feminine. The Isis cult spread from Egypt throughout the Middle East and Europe, reaching as far as Britain where remains of Isis temples have been found on Hadrian's Wall and in London. It is assumed that it was the Romans who named the river at its source as the Isis. Among her many attributes, Isis was a goddess of water, and choosing this name invokes all the depth and profound mysteries of this river.

The Celtic 1st century BCE Battersea Shield was dredged from the Thames mud in 1857. The original is in the British Musem.

Some of her many names give a sense of Isis, the all-encompassing goddess who has a multitude of gifts attributed to her: Goddess of Fertility, of Nature, of Motherhood, Lady of the Green Crops, Light Giver of Heaven, Lady of the Words of Power, Mother of the Gods, The One Who is All. Isis is the embodiment of all aspects of feminine divinity and wisdom, and has her counterpart in Sophia and the trinity of St Mary.

From earliest times, the Thames held a special place as England's most sacred and majestic river. It was revered by the Celts and Romans, and since medieval times was often dedicated to St Mary, Mother of God. Along the course of the river, more than fifty of the many churches and chapels are dedicated to Mary and for the most part these sacred places adjoin bridges that span the river.

Winding its silvery way through valleys that have grown prosperous beside the fertile waters, the Thames flows sweetly along through seven counties: Gloucestershire, Wiltshire, Oxfordshire, Berkshire, Bucking-hamshire, Surrey and Greater London. Gliding by boat along this part of

Sculpture of the god Tamesis looking downstream from Henley Bridge

the Thames is a beautiful journey through the graceful tranquillity of the English landscape. As we draw towards London, the river's features start to change dramatically. The influence of the vast generative energy of the tidal Thames becomes evident at Teddington, a derivative of Tide-End-Town. Then we enter the ten-mile stretch of water that takes us through the heart of London and onwards to meet the sea.

A Seat of Power

Sea-faring trade with Continental ports began in the Bronze Age and the Thames Valley became a leading trading area. Later, the Romans came to London and consolidated the city as an international port, building wharves, mills and the first crossing at London Bridge.

The seat of power has always been located on the river, whether it be the seat of royal sovereignty, of ecclesiastical power, of political power or the power of finance and commerce. All have established their centre on the river. From Windsor Palace in the west to the Tower of London in the east, the banks of the Thames were and are lined with royal palaces: Windsor, Hampton Court, Richmond, Whitehall, Bermondsey and the Tower of London. The Church housed the Archbishop of Canterbury at Lambeth Palace opposite the Palace of Westminster, the seat of the Houses of Parliament. The huge number of famous buildings gave rise to the description of the river as a string of pearls. In 1929 the Member of Parliament John Burns famously described the river as 'liquid history'.

From Pure Stream to Open Sewer

As the fortunes of the city grew, so the relationship between Londoners and the river changed. Love for the river grew cold. The once-beautiful silver Thames stank to high heaven as it became overwhelmed by the sheer volume of rubbish and effluent daily tipped into the water. Politicians in the Houses of Parliament debating the spoils of Empire could barely breathe as the stench of the Thames passed beneath their windows. Edmund Spenser's idyllic poem, written in 1596, conjures a picture of pure beauty: swans gliding on the silver streaming Thames, a flock of nymphs in the meadow, each one a bride. 'Sweet Thames, run softly, till I end my song!' Two hundred years later, the city is crowded and filthy, the river losing its wild beauty and becoming part of a tightly mapped city of ownership. As William Blake wrote in his 1794 poem 'London': 'I wander thro' each charter'd street, Near where the charter'd Thames does flow'.

The Tower of London with Tower Bridge

The nineteenth-century poet William Wordsworth feels the power of the river to redeem itself, despite the onslaught of human activity despoiling the water. But he is a romantic poet, writing from the Arcadian distance of Richmond in west London, where the riverside parkland echoed a more idyllic past.

> 'Glide gently, thus forever glide,
> O Thames! that other bards may see,
> As lovely visions by thy side
> As now, fair river! come to me.
> Oh glide, fair stream! for ever so;
> Thy quiet soul on all bestowing,
> 'Till all our minds forever flow,
> As thy deep waters now are flowing'.

The river at that time was so polluted that the lovely vision could only be seen in the mind's eye. The Thames became twice filthy, a fitting symbol for the moral and physical corruption of nineteenth-century London. In the call for change, great plans for cleaning up the river were drawn up. First, the embankments were built, made from granite brought from Cornwall, rather than concrete or metal. In defending the more expensive choice, a contemporary account describes how 'headland after headland' of granite 'standing out into the breakers' could be seen. Safely enclosing the river within solid boundaries, this ensured that the wild tidal waters were tamed. The embankments have the effect of making the river part of the built

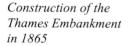

Construction of the Thames Embankment in 1865

environment, so bringing it into closer relationship with the city. Yet at the same time they separate the people from the river, placing it out of reach.

Once the embankments were in place, the next step was the construction of the London sewage system. This ambitious and costly scheme was designed by Joseph Bazalguette in response to the great stink of 1858, a particularly hot summer which made life in London unbearable. The plan entailed building a vast network of tunnels beneath London, some buried within embankments also designed by Bazalguette. He had the genius of foresight to double the size of the system so that, while modified and extended, it still serves London today. If we were to go down a manhole in Hampstead and knew which way to turn, we could walk for twenty miles and emerge in Beckton at the outfall tunnel. This new system was hailed as one of the seven wonders of the industrial world, carrying a number of unintended but welcome consequences including the elimination of cholera, which was caused by drinking contaminated water. Today, it is recognised that the Embankment is an essential part of the infrastructure needed to prevent the waters of London from inundating the city.

Slightly further downriver from where the Lea joins the Thames, the shimmering floodgates of the Thames Barrier protect London from flooding. 'Tamesis' is related to the flood-plain god Temavus, a name given to rivers that have a tendency to flood. Londoners carry a constant low-lying anxiety about the imminence of major flooding, and more so with rising sea-levels.

In the eleventh century, King Cnut (Canute) set up his throne on Thorney Island by the Thames and commanded the tide to stop, ostensibly to demonstrate the limits of his temporal power in the face of nature.

Coin of Cnut the Great

The Thames Barrier spans the river and protects the city from flooding

Currently, plans are being discussed to improve London's flood defences, plans which will literally determine the fate of the city. It may be that the mighty Thames will ultimately destroy the city that is her gift.

A New Era for London's Rivers

No longer a busy thoroughfare, the Thames glides quietly on. Modern Londoners have little contact with the river which was once so central to the everyday life of the city. Fifty years ago, the river was officially declared dead after many years of the worst possible polluting behaviour. T.S. Eliot's epic poem, *The Wasteland*, uses Spenser's poetic idyll as a way to convey the spiritually bankrupt wasteland of the twentieth century.

> 'The nymphs are departed.
> And their friends, the loitering heirs of city directors;
> Departed, have left no addresses.
> By the waters of Leman I sat down and wept
> Sweet Thames, run softly till I end my song,
> Sweet Thames, run softly, for I speak not loud or long'.

Yet we are now seeing a renewed connection with the river. It seems that Londoners are no longer hell-bent on destroying the Thames, even if the river ultimately rises up and inundates their city. Recently the Thames won awards for being the cleanest city river in the world, the result of years of work, planning and implementing new ways to manage the watercourse. Children have sewn a Thames tapestry for the Olympics. Each year, there is a Thames Festival, and numerous local interest groups have the Thames as their focus.

Today, Londoners are increasingly involved in uncovering their lost rivers. Some local communities have done clearing work with sections of river, creating parkland areas where the water can emerge and flow freely. Elsewhere, there are grander plans including one to turn Fleet Street, which crosses the route of the old River Fleet, into a Venetian-style waterway. How Christopher Wren would smile!

We have seen that London's historic rise to power as Britain's capital city has developed along the Thames. With their shared history, discovering Thames the river is one of the best ways to get to know London the city. How much is the Thames an expression of London, at the heart of this great city's *genius loci* or spirit of place? After all the busy times past, the relative silence upon the Thames begs some serious questions. It is as though the Thames with its powerful generative energy awaits a new call. From where this might come from or where it will take us is not yet apparent. Like the bards, poets and shamans of the past, when we seek answers to such questions, we can always go down to the river. As we gaze down upon and listen to the waters, the Thames may offer up an answer.

The River by Moonlight by Henry Pether who was active between 1828-1862

The London Dragon at Temple Bar

DRAGON CITY:
A VIEW OF SACRED LONDON

Peter Dawkins

Considered a sacred city for millennia, London is also known as a Dragon City, its heraldic creature being a dragon. As in most heraldry, this emblem was chosen because that is how the city was perceived symbolically. The question is why? To understand this we need to understand the landscape and the geocosmological awareness of those who founded and developed the city. We also need to appreciate the knowledge of these things as passed on in the specialised yet universal language of symbolism and myth.

To understand the landscape we need to imagine what it was like before all the buildings were constructed upon it, most especially before the modern city sprawled over it in all directions. Developed over the centuries on the foundations and site of the original city, the heart of the present-day metropolis is the City of London. This is still defined as it was centuries ago by the outline of the walls built by the Romans, with an outer boundary. According to legend, this city is very ancient and existed in some form or other long before the Romans conquered the land and rebuilt London to their own taste.

The Founding of London

According to tradition, London was first founded as a city or settlement by Brit (Roman: Brutus), a descendant of Aeneas and the Trojans from whom the Brythonic Celts (i.e. Britons or British) take their name. 'Brit' means 'Chosen', and is a name or title which was probably bestowed because he was chosen by the Oracle in his vision to lead his followers to the land that subsequently became known as Britain. Because of the Trojan link, pre-Roman London was referred to as Caer Troia ('Seat of Troy') or Nova Troia ('New Troy').

Brit founded London in the traditional way, by finding and marking the geomantic centre with a stone. Such a stone is the 'foundation stone', sometimes called an omphalos. It is the geodesic heart-stone and signifies the central pillar or *Axis Mundi* around which everything else revolves and from which all measurements of distance are made. This particular Stone is known as the London Stone or Brutus Stone, and until recently all distances from London were calculated from this Stone. Only a fragment of it still exists and this has been set into the street wall of the building that occupies the site of St Swithin London Stone, a church that was bombed in the War. Originally the Stone was much larger, some say as large as a man, and stood just in front of what is now Cannon Street Station, the site of which, in Roman times, was occupied by a palace. Needless to say, the placing of such an important stone would have been done very carefully and significantly. Three millennia ago, when this is supposed to have happened, the site would almost certainly have been in its natural state.

The site chosen was certainly special. The Stone was set up in the middle of virtually the only high ground that borders the River Thames in the centre of a great flat plain known as the Thames Basin. This high ground consists of three low-lying hills known to us today as Ludgate Hill, Corn Hill and Tower Hill. These form the southern end of a ridge extending southwards from much higher hills that line the northern rim of the Thames Basin. One could imagine this ridge as a creature coming forward out of the northern hills to drink at the water's edge of the River Thames – a dragon perhaps? The west side of this ridge was clearly defined by the River Fleet (now channelled underground), originally a large river that hosted a port at the foot of Ludgate Hill in Saxon and later times, and perhaps earlier times too. The east side of the ridge, below Tower Hill, consisted of low-lying marshy land. Flowing southwards down the centre of the ridge and into the Thames was a little river called, from Roman times onwards, the Wall Brook. This is also now piped underground, but originally flowed in a steep-sided valley, now filled in. The London Stone was erected on a high point above the east bank of this brook and north bank of the Thames.

Chakric Energy Centres in the Landscape

Before describing the Dragon City of London it is useful to introduce the idea of the landscape temple system and how it affects and is used by human beings, either knowingly or intuitively, in the layout and use of towns and cities. London happens to be a particularly good example. A temple can be defined as an expression of a divine archetype, idea or spirit that is holistic – that is, complete in itself and therefore holy. The human form, for instance, is one such example, which is why it is traditionally referred to as the temple of the spirit or temple of the soul or even temple of God. As a temple, the human body is composed of three major parts – the head, the chest and the abdomen – which work together, need each other and form a trinity-in-unity that expresses the idea of the Holy Trinity. These three parts are linked together by the spine. Lying

The Three Areas and Seven Chakras of the Human Body

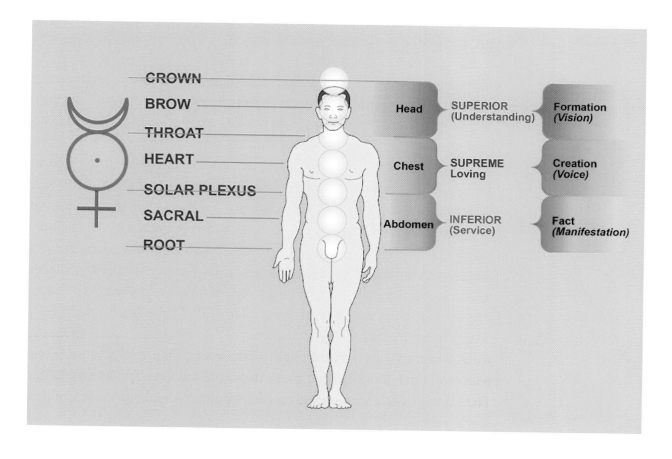

along the spine are seven major chakras or energy centres. In India, teachings about these seven chakras always have been readily available, but in the West, although there has been knowledge of these energy foci, it has been kept a guarded secret, veiled in allegory and symbolism. That there should be seven such foci can be understood geometrically. If you link three circles (representing head, chest and abdomen) that touch each other with an axis (spine) through the centres, seven focal points are created along the axis as a result. These seven focal points are the three centres of the circles, the two places where the upper and lower circles touch the middle circle, and the very top and bottom of the axis where it extends to the nadir of the lower circle and the crown of the higher circle. In the human form, the chakras at the centres of the head, chest and abdomen are known as the brow, heart and sacral chakras respectively. The chakra situated between the head and chest is called the throat chakra, and the chakra between the chest and abdomen is named the solar plexus chakra. The crown chakra is at the top of the head and the root chakra is at the base of the spine.

Just as the whole human form is a body of energy and consciousness, so each of these chakric centres is the focus of a particular type of energy and consciousness related to its position in the body. The seven chakras are linked to each other by an energy carried by the spine. Because of the nature of polarity (i.e. between crown and root) this energy is dual in nature and operation, manifesting as two separate and different energy flows, one descending from the crown to the root and the other ascending from the root to the crown. The descending energy is described metaphorically as a lightning flash or spear of light, because it is straight in form like a ray of light. The ascending energy, which responds to the descending one, is a spiralling energy, symbolised as a serpent or dragon. In the Vedic tradition the latter is called the kundalini, whilst in the British tradition it is called the dragon.

However, this model of subtle chakric energies is not only found in the temple of the human body. It is also replicated in the design of buildings such as cathedrals, churches and temples, although one can also find the archetypal pattern and energy flow in most traditional townscapes and ordinary homes, as the chakras form a natural sequence of activity areas. This fundamental archetype can also be found in the natural landscape, hence the name 'landscape temple'.

When a natural landscape temple can be recognised, it becomes easier to design and build towns and cities in harmony with nature, each helping and enhancing the other. All over the world there are examples of such townscapes, where key buildings such as churches, palaces, marketplaces, government buildings and the like have been sited on appropriate energy points that are conducive to the type of activity taking place in the building and that specific part of the town or city. Often such townscapes have grown naturally, organically or instinctively to this archetypal design, as the archetype is inherent in nature and life generally, whilst sometimes they have been consciously and deliberately designed to express the archetype by knowledgeable architects, patrons and builders.

The axis of a town or city does not have to follow a straight line like the human spine. Indeed, it may more often be crooked or sinuous, but whatever its path, it is vitally important that polarities exist. The greater the polarity, the more energized the place can be – for instance, such as when the head area is on a hill and the root area is in a valley, near a river or lake.

In an ideal townscape, the heart centre should be a place of peace, harmony and beauty reflecting the psychological nature of the heart. The throat area, being the centre of intelligence as well as of speaking and listening, is ideally suited for schools, libraries, theatres and concert halls. The brow chakra is usually associated with administrative buildings such as offices. Markets and shopping areas, the great centres of commerce and trade, function best in the solar plexus area, as also do restaurants, pubs and other eating places. Industries and workshops, and all things associated with material creativity, function well in the sacral chakra (as do red light areas!), while activities involving distribution, storage and protection naturally belong to the root chakra area.

There is always some local variation in the chakric landscape scheme and these energy centres are not absolutely binding in their role and function in order for a city to thrive and be successful, especially as

A silver dragon of London in the Leadenhall Market

smaller chakra systems can exist within each chakra of a larger system, enabling complexity to naturally flourish. Bearing that in mind, let us now see how this natural energy system is manifested and utilised in the development of London as a city set on the River Thames.

Laying out the Chakric Dragon Temple

We can see how the Britons recognised a landscape temple on which they laid out a 'townscape temple' stretching from east to west along the three hills bordering the Thames. Having marked a heart centre, the next main focal points to mark are the crown and root centres.

The crown centre is the summit of Ludgate Hill, the name of which is derived from the British god Lud (Lludd), equivalent to the Greek god Zeus and Roman god Jupiter, associated with heaven and the crown chakra. Lud is also the name of the third of 'The Three Pillars of Britain'

The chakric system in Celto-Roman London

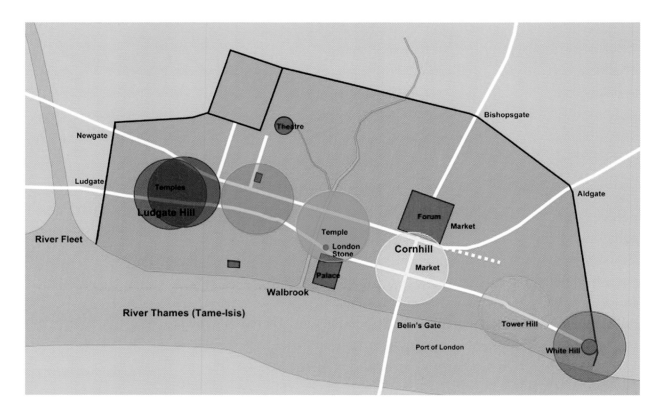

(Brit, Molmutius and Lud) and he is recognised as the third founder of London who, in the eighth century BCE, reputedly built defensive towers all around the city and fine homes for the people. When he died his body was buried near the west gateway of the city, thereafter named Ludgate (*Porthlud* in Welsh). The Britons supposedly created a temple or sanctuary on the summit of Ludgate Hill dedicated to the goddess Arianrhod, the feminine counterpart to Lud and equivalent to Hera of the Greeks and Juno of the Romans. This sanctuary was also associated with Arianrhod's son, the sun-god Lleu, who was metamorphosed by poets into the legendary King Arthur. The Romans replaced the British sanctuary with a temple to Diana and another to Jupiter. The site is now occupied by St Paul's Cathedral, so-called because St Paul preached here in Roman times. This is as the story is told nowadays, although in fact 'St Paul' is actually a corruption of 'St Pole', who originally was not a saint but an upright pole or stone planted on the crown of the hill – ostensibly the original stone out of which Arthur drew the sword to prove his worthiness to be king. Possibly in commemoration of King Lud, or perhaps in dedication to the god Lud, the city was given the name Caer Lud.

Whilst the crown chakra in a landscape temple is associated with the highest point, the root chakra is normally associated with the lowest point and, if possible, water. The site chosen for this is on the east side of Tower Hill, at the foot of the hill. In this low-lying area, washed by the Thames, the Britons created a small hill or mound known as the White Mound (*Bryn Gwynt* in Welsh). Later, the Norman king William the Conqueror constructed the White Tower, known also as the Tower of London, on top of the mound. This ancient mound was a burial mound, at least symbolically if not actually, in which is reputedly buried the head of the great god Bran together with the heads and bodies of Brit, the founder of Britain, and Molmutius, the great lawgiver, whose laws gave the people basic freedoms such as the right to free speech and to be deemed innocent unless proven guilty – the foundation of British Common Law. There is not much to see of this mound nowadays, as the ground all around has been raised and reformed over the centuries.

A burial mound on the water's edge is a good symbol for a root chakra.

The White Tower from a fifteenth-century manuscript

The Coat of Arms of the City of London. The motto reads 'Lord Guide Us'.

It equates to the underworld of classical mythology. In British and other traditions it is also associated with the cave or lair of the dragon, equivalent to the coiled kundalini of Hindu Tantric tradition. This is the dragon that human St George or the archangel Michael confronts and pierces with his spear of light. The spear signifies wisdom, the dragon intelligence. In British mythology, the equivalent of St George and the archangel Michael, his divine counterpart, is King Arthur and the sun-god Lleu respectively. Lleu's wife or feminine counterpart is Blodeuwedd, the magically-created daughter of Gwydion, the original Merlin. She is *Gwen-ouivre* (Guinevere), meaning 'the White Dragon'. The story of Lleu and Blodeuwedd's feisty relationship is the basis of the later Arthur-Guinevere story, and is an allegory of the two polarities of life and their interactions. Guinevere is the Celtic equivalent of the Hindu goddess Kundalini, a natural expression of the Shakti of Shiva. Geomantically, she is what is known as the earth-energy consciousness.

As well as the Red Cross, signifying the radiance of light, Arthur's chief heraldic emblem was the Red Dragon, now the emblem of Wales. As a war-leader, he was known as the Pendragon ('Head of the Dragon'), the title given to all royal British war-leaders. Allegorically, the spear or sword of light symbolises the magnetic ray of spiritual light that descends the body from the crown chakra to the root, where it attracts and draws up the dragon energy or kundalini from root to crown. When this dragon energy is fully raised it produces illumination. This process is enacted in sacred ritual, such as Holy Communion or Mass, in a temple architecturally designed to simulate the human body. The same design in its essence underlies a landscape temple, as it is a basic spiritual archetype that underlies all life forms. It is a skill, however, to raise the dragon from root to crown and produce illumination. It can be and is done through the liturgy of the church, and also through pilgrimage in the landscape. The White Mound with the Tower on it is associated with the sovereignty of the land. Any would-be sovereign of the land has to first possess the Tower. This empowers the sovereign. Publicly this is explained as the need to possess the Tower so as to protect the citizens of London and the sovereign, which for a period of time was a practical reality. However, the

GUARDIANS OF THE SACRED CITY

Chris Street

On either side of London, etched into the landscape by the courses of roads, rivers, paths, hedgerows and fields, are the outlines of two huge creatures. One resembles a seated, sphinx-like lion, facing due east; the other is a reasonable likeness of a unicorn, complete with single horn, facing west.

Once noticed, their outlines can be made out on most maps as well as on the aerial photography of Google Earth. They are vast. Both creatures are over nine miles from tip to tail. Their heads are most readily recognisable and where their haunches merge into the urban sprawl of Greater London both figures become less well-defined.

Their existence raises a number of questions: who, what, why, where and how being just a few of them. As the person who first noticed these images, I have some ideas about their origins and significance, which arise from the circumstances of their discovery.

One contributory factor could be the human brain's built-in tendency to recognise familiar patterns and shapes in unusual places. That's why people can see faces and figures in the grain of a wooden door, the contours of craggy facial features in outcrops of rock, or the image of Jesus in a piece of burnt toast. This phenomenon is called simulacra.

However, these two figures do not seem to be as random as the usual simulacra. It is clear we're not dealing with a single image here, but with a pair of images which are meaningfully related. They normally stand together on the royal crest as the heraldic guardians of British sovereignty. Here, they stand either side of the capital city, London, an arrangement

The natural markings on the fishtail spell out in Arabic letters, 'There is no God but God'

A native North American profile stares out to the Rocky Mountains

entirely in keeping with their roles.

To diminish the possibility of coincidence further, the two images form a meaningful part of a remarkable discovery known as the London Earthstars Matrix. It also is emblazoned upon the London landscape but in a different way to the Lion and Unicorn. Yet all three are fundamentally connected.

To grasp the role of the Lion and Unicorn properly, you'll need a brief explanation of the Earthstars discovery. Basically, it reveals that London's ancient sacred sites are not located around the capital at random, but connect in a vast and complex geometric pattern. This Matrix includes many old parish churches and sacred hills as well as obvious places such as Westminster Abbey, St Paul's Cathedral, Southwark Cathedral and the Tower of London.

In all, there are nineteen designs, mostly pentagrams, hexagrams, circles and triangles. None of them are separate. Every single one is connected to the rest as part of a composite whole.

The significance of the Earthstars Matrix is partially revealed by the nature of the design itself. It is a recognisable temple ground plan, but on a vast scale, covering over four hundred square miles of Greater London.

The Pantheon in Rome is built upon an almost identical design, whilst the oldest British temple to utilise this geometry in its layout is Stonehenge, whose circles of megaliths were erected over 3500 years ago. It's astonishing to think that concealed within London's landscape is a giant plan of Stonehenge, defined by the stones of London's oldest churches and cathedrals rather than the bluestones and sarsens of the henge itself.

Even more surprising is that the work of the late John Michell, who was probably the world's leading scholar of these arcane subjects, demonstrates unequivocally that the London Earthstars geometry bears a very meaningful relationship to the measures and proportions of the biblical City of Revelation, the New Jerusalem.

In the context of the Earthstars discovery, the guardians of the holy city stand either side of this hidden temple and relate to the inner spiritual dimension of the London landscape more than its physical counterpart, the bustling, overpopulated, materialistic capital of our country.

They are guardians of an inner temple and holy city concealed within the physical.

They also represent two polarities, which in the mystery traditions are often described as the pillars of the temple. The Lion represents a solar, male, kingly energy: the active principle. The Unicorn represents a lunar, intuitive energy, linked to the divine feminine principle.

Through many examples of synchronistic connections, the landscape figures demonstrate clear and undeniable links to these archetypal polarities, often in a quite startling way, so let's take a closer look at them.

*The Royal Coat of Arms
of the United Kingdom
with supporting
Lion and Unicorn*

The History of the Heraldic Beasts

The Royal Crest evolved over the past nine hundred years and in its first form was simply three lions, used by Richard the Lionheart as a heraldic device. The version using the Lion and the Unicorn is a relatively modern creation, historically speaking. It came into existence when James VI of Scotland became James I of England in 1603 and represented a merger of two previous heraldic emblems: the Lion of England and the Unicorn of Scotland. The features that define these figures upon the landscape appear to be much older and remarkably, would have been

The Lion King image guarding the east of London

visible only from the air.

Similar figures associated with landscape zodiacs were, in the past, assumed to have been ancient constructions which deteriorated over the centuries. I don't believe this to be the case. My personal opinion is that they are an expression of what might be termed 'the spirit of place' and have evolved over a long period of time, often unwittingly added to by humanity.

Having worked with these phenomena for many years, I think the evidence supports this perspective, but I am aware that many people might disagree or formulate other theories.

In order to better understand my perspective, it is worthwhile to take a closer look at these remarkable figures emblazoned upon the landscape.

The Lion King Image

The head, back and mane of the Lion is defined by various features, including the A113 road from Passingford Bridge and Chigwell to Woodford. Meandering alongside it virtually all the way is the river Roding, adding a curly mane. The Lion's face follows the B175 road from Passingford Bridge through Stapleford Abbotts to Romford. The eye is in the area of Battles Hall and St Mary's Stapleford. The Lion's mouth is in the area of Havering at Bower, and its chest is the A112 through Chadwell Heath. The paws rest comfortably in Dagenham defined by parts of the A125 and A1112.

The kingly stature of the lion is emphasised by the surprising fact that some of the old paths, tracks and boundary lines above its head can actually be linked up in the shape of a very regal-looking crown, remarkably similar to the one on the real crest.

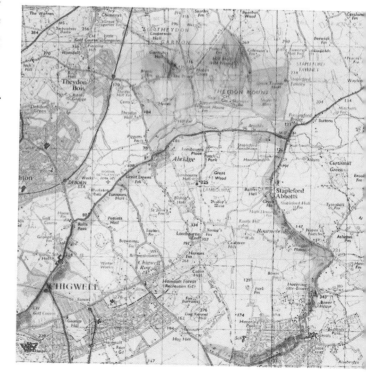

The Lion's crown at Theydon Mount in the Essex countryside

The River of the Sun King

In mythology, the lion is always regarded as a regal beast, linked to the sun and widely regarded as the king of the jungle. On the Essex landscape, those attributes are revealed in more than just the Lion image. They are also present as fundamental associations with other landscape features, most notably the River Lea which flows across the back of the Lion and through its shanks.

The name of the River Lea derives from the ancient Celtic sun god, Lugh, the shining one. As if to emphasise this, its source is in Luton (Lugh's Town). The spring is actually within an earthwork enclosure known as Waulud's Bank and is a mark point on the famous St Michael Ley, also known as the Michael Mary Line.

To confirm the unusual connection between the river, the sun god Lugh and the landscape Lion, in Welsh (the original language of the ancient British peoples), *lleu* means 'lion'. So the attributes of the ancient river of the sun god mirror those of the solar Lion on the Essex landscape, through which it flows.

Lugh's river rises in Luton, flows through Hertford and Ware and then down through East London to enter the Thames just east of the Isle of Dogs. Just below Temple Mills (formerly important holdings of the Knights Templar), it loops around the 2012 Stratford Olympic Stadium like a moat around a sacred enclosure.

Can it be mere coincidence that there is the image of a solar Lion here on the landscape where our ancestors named the river after a solar hero or sun god? Or that on the opposite side of London stands a huge image, not of the sun, but of its lunar counterpart, the moon goddess?

The Unicorn

Like the Lion, the Unicorn has an outline defined by a combination of roads, pathways and rivers. The horse-like back and mane is defined by the A410 Uxbridge Road, and the rear end by parts of the A1 and A41. It's especially worth noting that the tip of the short horn is a place actually

The Unicorn image guards the west of London

called Horn Hill, near Maple Cross, where there is a small, pleasant Victorian chapel dedicated to St Paul.

The head of the Unicorn is defined by the rivers of the area, principally the Colne and the Ver. In mythology, the Unicorn has a special relationship to the virgin moon goddess. One legend states that the unicorn rests its head on the lap of the goddess, and on the London landscape it actually does. The head of the Unicorn rests upon the course of several rivers with distinct goddess associations.

To our remote ancestors, all rivers were perceived to be living entities inhabited by deific spirits, mostly feminine river goddesses. Sabrina, for example, was the goddess of the Severn. The Ver takes its name from a little-known ancient British goddess. It is believed her name relates to the old Welsh word, *fair* (there is no 'v' in old Welsh), which today means Mary. *Llanfair*, for example, means sacred place of Mary. So it appears that the goddess Ver and the Christian Mary are connected.

Like the sacred waters rising in the shadow of Glastonbury Tor, the River Ver has a red spring and a white spring, which rise at Redbourne and Markyate respectively. The Ver runs into the Colne north of Watford and stretches along the entire west side of London through Rickmansworth, Uxbridge, Denham and finally into the Thames at Staines.

So the whole of London is enclosed by sacred rivers. On the north, north-east and east, the river is of the sun god Lugh. On the north-west and west, are the goddess rivers of the Unicorn. Of course, they both join the Thames which carries both polarities, since on old maps it is shown as Thames-Isis or Tamesis. This name also reflects the principal god and goddess, Tammuz and Ishtar (Isis), of those inveterate mariners, the Phoenicians, who are known to have travelled to these islands.

The Sacred Leys

Two of the most important ley alignments of the capital pass through the Earthstars' Lion and Unicorn and remarkably, their associations again suggest similar influences.

Running through the Lion is a royal ley line which combines a solar energy path (directly aligned to the midsummer sunrise) with some remarkable connections to the sovereignty of the land and the notion of kingship; features entirely in keeping with the attributes of the regal leonine figure.

By contrast, the Unicorn has an appropriate alignment of churches linked to the divine feminine. Most of its churches are dedicated to St Mary, who is often depicted standing on a crescent moon. She is the Christian incarnation of the virgin moon goddess archetype.

These leys, like the Lion and Unicorn images, each represent a power in the land linked to the original notion of divine sovereignty, which can be seen as the rule of the Grail Kings and Queens.

The Coronation Line

The Lion's ley has been called the Coronation Line. It runs diagonally through the entire figure up to the area of its forehead and crown. As previously mentioned, the lion is commonly associated both with the sun and the concept of kingship, as does this alignment.

Part of the Coronation Line, probably London's most significant ley line, showing the Kingston Stone, St Paul's Cathedral and Westminster Abbey

It's a midsummer sunrise alignment which passes through London's two most important sacred sites, St Paul's Cathedral and Westminster Abbey. Basically, that means on midsummer's morn, the sun will rise and shine its first beams directly along this axis: an apparently perfect confirmation of a direct link. These days, a few office blocks would need to be demolished to make the sunrise from St Paul's visible, but in the past there would likely have been a clear view.

The ley-line's connections to sovereignty are equally impressive. I gave it the name the Coronation Line since it passes through places which have been linked to the coronation rites of our monarchs for over a thousand years.

One such place it the King Stone at Kingston-upon-Thames, upon which seven Saxon kings received their crown. The second coronation site is the Collegiate Church of St Peter, better known as Westminster Abbey, where Kings and Queens from William of Normandy onwards have been crowned, the only exceptions being Edward V and Edward VIII.

The third site on the Coronation Line is, surprisingly, St Paul's Cathedral, where in medieval times an open-air moot was regularly held in the churchyard. This may have evolved from a druidic open-air parliament, and one of its functions was to provide a vote on the successor to the crown by the peers and the people. Edward IV, Stephen, Edward the Confessor, Edmund Ironsides and several other monarchs are on record as having submitted to this traditional procedure. The last king to do so was Henry III in 1216.

Some of the other mark points on this ley are: St George's Hill at Weybridge (site of a hill fort), Whiteley's Village, Wayneflete's Manor (remains of an eleventh-century bishop's palace), the King Stone, St Stephen's Rochester Row, Westminster Abbey, St Margaret's Westminster, St Andrews-by-the-Wardrobe (the patron saint of Ikea?), the site of Blackfriar's monastery, St Paul's Cathedral, St Vedast at Foster Lane, St Mary Aldermanbury in Love Lane, the site of St John's Priory Holywell and the 'Mount' Arnold Circus.

From central London, the alignment passes through the entire length of the Lion's body to the crown of the beast near the Maypole Pub at

Chigwell Row, where it actually follows the course of the road leading to the crossroads, both of which would have been regarded by Alfred Watkins as valid ley mark points.

To add weight to the ley's royal connections, the folk moot at St Paul's is said to have been started by King Arthur. In Morte D'Arthur, Sir Thomas Mallory clearly suggests that Arthur pulled his sword of kingship from a stone in St Paul's churchyard, which I believe to have been the site of another King Stone on this alignment. One intriguing possibility is that this King Stone standing in the shadow of St Paul's was later moved to Candlewick Street where by the tenth century it became identified as the traditional London Stone of Brutus.

Meanwhile, on the other side of the capital, there's a mirror image of this Coronation Line, right through the body of the Unicorn to its horn. I've called it London's Mary Line.

London's Mary Line

In central London, the capital's Mary Line commences at St Mary-le-Strand in the middle of the Aldwych one-way system, where the line crosses Alfred Watkins' well-documented Strand Ley. A church has stood near this spot since Saxon times and it was the site of London's most popular Maypole, suggesting a pagan ritual site. The current building, designed by James Gibbs, dates from the early 1700s and is said to be the finest example of a Baroque interior in London.

The next Mary site on the line is the grand St Mary-le-Bone where the alignment appears to pass not only through the present church on Marylebone Road, but also through its former site around the corner in Marylebone Lane, where the Elizabethan philosopher Sir Francis Bacon was married in 1606.

The third Mary site on the alignment is the Shrine of Our Lady of Willesden, now the Parish Church of St. Mary Magdalene at Willesden Green. This is a very ancient and important place of pilgrimage and healing, having both a holy well and a Black Madonna. The well still flows for visitors to sample or take away its curative waters, but sadly, the Black

St Mary-le-Strand, in Aldwych, the start of London's Mary Line

Madonna is a reproduction since Oliver Cromwell viciously burnt the original in the seventeenth century.

There are also several places along this alignment which are not dedicated to St Mary. The ancient church of St Giles-in-the-fields, now at the end of Denmark Street, St Augustine's Kilburn Park Road (near the site of Kilburn Priory) and the Queen's House Greenwich, designed by Inigo Jones and formerly the site of a royal palace.

However, at the heart of the Unicorn and its alignment is one of the most important Mary churches in London, St Mary the Virgin at Harrow-on-the-Hill. The alignment actually seems to go through the school chapel and the summit of the hill, rather than the actual church, but it has clearly been a high place of the gods since long before Christian times. The earliest recorded church here dates from 1059 and 'The Grove' next to it suggests druidic origins, causing John Michell to form the opinion that a druidic college had existed here.

The Heart of the Unicorn

In my considered opinion, Harrow-on-the-Hill is the actual heart of the Unicorn and therefore a very important energy centre for the capital. It's also at the heart of its own sacred landscape, since Harrow's St Mary the Virgin lies at the centre of a pentagram of leys and sacred hills.

The sites that define Harrow's five-point star are Horsendon Hill (also a point of the larger Earthstars star pentagram), Barn Hill in Wembley, Belmont Hill in Stanmore, Dabb's Hill in Ruislip and St John's in Pinner. This is not quite a perfect pentagram. The sites radiate around Harrow, each at precisely 72 degrees but all at slightly different distances from the church.

Like the rest of the Earthstars geometries, the Harrow pentagram does not stand in isolation. Its alignments and sites all connect to the larger Earthstars geometry which covers the whole of London.

So what does the Harrow pentagram represent? Long before all the satanic and black magic associations, the five-point star has been a symbol of the feminine mysteries, as instanced by the mysteries of the goddess of

St Mary the Virgin at Harrow-on-the-Hill

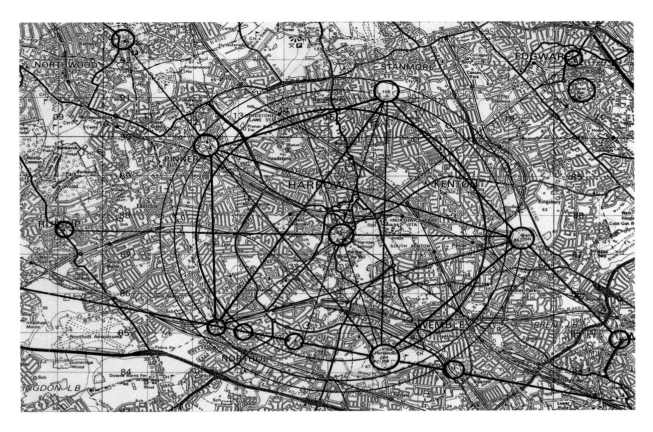

wisdom. Her planet Venus circumscribes a perfect five-pointed star in the night sky over a period of eight years. The pentagram was also the symbol of the Pythagorean mystery school and, far from being a symbol of dark practices, was placed on doors to ward off evil and to bring good luck.

The Harrow Pentagram, with the spire of St Mary the Virgin at Harrow on the Hill at the heart of the Unicorn

Most interesting is the connection of the pentagram to the source of Dan Brown's success, the best-selling book The Holy Blood and Holy Grail. The starting point for the mysteries unravelled in The Holy Blood and Holy Grail was the church of St Mary Magdalene at Rennes le Chateau in France. This church was found to be at the centre of a circle of hilltops and other sites which inscribed a pentagram on the landscape, just like at Harrow. Henry Lincoln's later books on the subject describe it as a vast temple to the goddess.

Now we have to ask, what does all this mean for London?

Is London under Divine Protection?

It appears that the Earthstars discovery strongly suggests that London has a hidden spiritual dimension: that its individual sacred sites, holy hills and other special places can be linked to form a complex geometric pattern which is a recognisable temple ground-plan.

In my opinion, this can be compared to a wiring diagram of the fundamental forces of creation that subtly empower all life upon this small planet. As such, it represents the hidden unity that connects all things, all religions, all people, at all levels. The arts and sciences evolving from it formed the basis of most mystery schools and traditions, and the secret knowledge of the temple builders. Though originating in pre-Christian times, in Christian terms it is best described as a science of the Holy Spirit.

That these hidden forces form a particularly powerful energy centre in

*The Unicorn with
its heart at
Harrow on the Hill*

our capital city adds another dimension to the idea that it is a focus of world power, but perhaps not in the way we would normally imagine. Is it evolving into a spiritual centre, a holy city? The mystically-inclined already regard it as a planetary chakra – a powerful vortex of spiritual energy.

Moreover, there has always been a tradition that considered Britain as occupying a special place in the world, based upon the concepts of fair play, truth and justice, and related to its destiny as the Grail Kingdom.

To the average person in these times, these ideas may be difficult to acknowledge. Even I find it extraordinary that the heraldic guardians of Britain, the Lion and the Unicorn, stand etched into the landscape either side of London. Nevertheless, they are definitely there, and are now emerging into human awareness and consciousness while suggesting that the capital may be under some form of divine protection.

It would appear that we are dealing with the appearance of profoundly mythical creatures: a unicorn and something closely resembling C.S. Lewis' great lion, Aslan.

Perhaps, therefore, something far more magical is afoot.

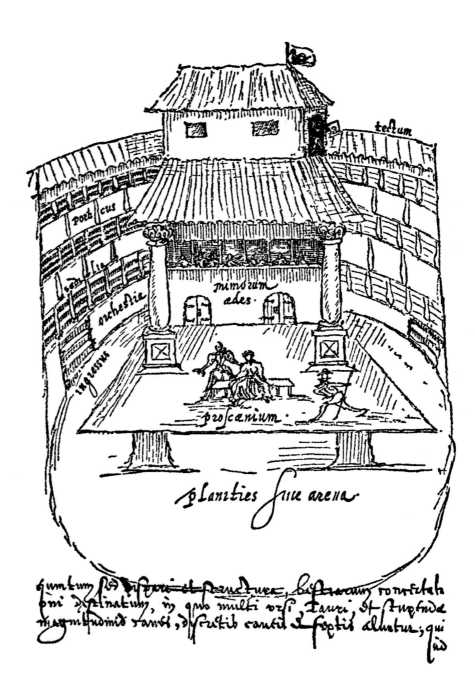

*The stage of the
Swan Theatre
built in 1595*

SHAKESPEARE, THE SWAN AND ELIZABETHAN THEATRE

Peter Dawkins

The Temple Theatre and Mysteries

London is world-renowned for its culture and for its theatre in particular. Pre-eminent and most widely known amongst all the theatrical achievements in both London's and the nation's history is that of Shakespeare, although he is not alone. The reasons for this are as diverse as they are simple, with talent playing but a part in the whole story. Behind it all is knowledge of secret or sacred things, and the Mysteries.

Theatres have a long history of being associated with sacred matters. The earliest theatres belonged to the classical Mystery Schools, wherein sacred drama was performed in the temples for the education and initiation of neophytes. When it developed into a more public form of theatre, the drama was still associated with the sacred Mysteries. The English word 'Mysteries' is derived from the Greek word *mysteria*, which denoted the sacred drama enacted in the Ancient Orphic, Greek and later Roman Mystery Schools. The mystics (Greek, *mystes*) were those who experienced these Mysteries.

The idea of the Mysteries was to provide a dramatic experience that engaged all the senses, in which the emotions would be moved and the mind enlightened. The Mysteries themselves were allegories containing not only a mixture of history, fable, legend and symbolism but also profound wisdom. They portrayed the fundamental path of life which all human beings tread to some extent or other and the various levels of attainment that the soul can reach, including how to reach those levels and the kind of challenges or tests to be encountered and overcome. The path was and still is called the path of initiation. The Mysteries were continued within Christianity, in terms of both the theatrical nature of church service and also plays that portray the Christian version of the ancient sacred story. The Eucharist is still known as a Mystery and plays based upon the stories of the Bible that were performed regularly either in churches or by travelling players in the medieval era were known as the Mystery Plays. The medieval Guilds also had their own Mysteries, of which the Freemasonic Mystery was to be developed to a high art during the Shakespeare period. Elizabethan theatre was heir to this heritage and tradition.

Elizabethan Playhouses

The Rose Theatre, misnamed as The Globe, from Visscher's View of London, 1616

The first purpose-built Elizabethan outdoor playhouses had simple names related to the theatre, such as The Theatre (built 1576) and The Curtain (built 1577). But from the late 1580s onwards, the names of the new playhouses were all associated with classical symbolism and the Mysteries: e.g. The Rose (built 1587), The Swan (built 1595), The Globe (built 1599) and The Fortune (built 1600). Clearly by design, these six theatres relate to each other by name in couples:

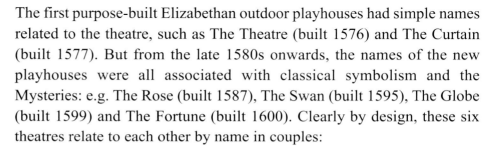

> The Theatre and The Curtain have names belonging purely to play house terminology.

> The Rose and The Swan have names drawn from the Orphic tradition – Orpheus being represented as a singing swan or as a rose, and being known as the refounder not only of the Mysteries but also of the Society of the original Rosy Cross.

> The Globe and The Fortune are twinned in the symbolic representation of the goddess Fortune who stands upon the globe of the world.

The Globe Theatre from Hollar's View of London, 1647

As recently confirmed by the research of Joy Hancox into the Byrom Collection of drawings that were once the prized possession of an eighteenth-century secret society, the Elizabethan theatres were built according to a plan and designs originating from a group of people who formed a secret society knowledgeable in the Mysteries and the cabala of number, geometry, sound, symbolism and architecture that accompanied them. One needs to add to this the knowledge of townscape and landscape temples, as we shall see. Notable amongst them were the royal astrologer

Dr John Dee, the Earl of Leicester, the influential philosopher Francis Bacon and the noble families of the Sidneys and the Pembrokes. The Pembrokes and Bacon, together with the Earls of Essex and Southampton and a few others, formed what is known as 'the Shakespeare Circle'.

In 1594, two great acting companies – the Lord Chamberlain's Men and the Lord Admiral's Men – were formed out of various amalgamations of previous companies, and these two thereafter dominated the Elizabethan stage. The latter set up home in The Rose, whilst the former established themselves at The Theatre. The Rose was situated in Bankside, Southwark, on the south side of the River Thames, whilst The Theatre was located in Shoreditch, just outside and north of the City of London. In 1598, by decree of the Privy Council, these two were the only acting companies allowed

A map of Tudor London showing the sites of the main theatres

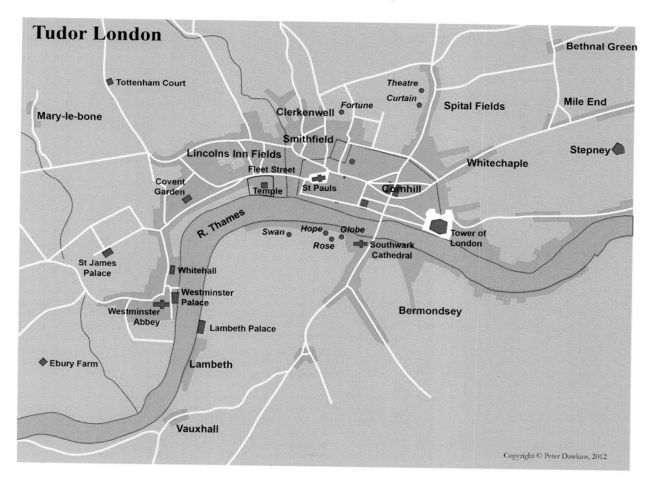

to perform in London for the next twenty-five years. In 1599, the Lord Chamberlain's Men dismantled the Theatre and moved it south across the Thames to Bankside, where they re-erected it and renamed it The Globe. They were followed soon after, in 1600, by the Lord Admiral's Men who moved north across the Thames and occupied the Fortune Theatre, newly-built in the parish of St Giles-without-Cripplegate, just outside the City of London and west of the site of The Theatre.

The Fortune and The Globe

The Globe and The Fortune theatres were built within a year of each other. The builders of The Fortune were instructed to follow the design of The Globe in all respects, except that The Fortune was to be square instead of circular. Unless one knows the secret of squaring the circle and the meaning behind it, this seems to be not only an impossible task but a meaningless instruction. However, the classical, medieval and renaissance architects (master builders) knew this secret.

The squaring of the circle is achieved when a square is created whose perimeter equals in measurement the circumference of the circle it is

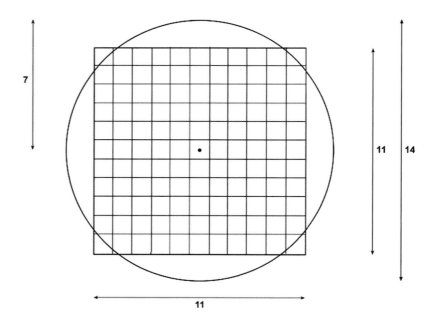

The meaning of Squaring the Circle was one of the inner secrets of sacred design

squaring; or, alternatively, whose area is the same as the area of the circle. It is a philosophical metaphor for the loving union of two complete opposites in a harmony of equality and beauty. Known as the Mystical Marriage in this inner tradition, it is particularly used as a metaphor for the marriage of spirit and matter, heaven and earth, immortality and mortality, wisdom and intelligence, intuitive heart and rational mind, or the union of imagination and reason. It is understood that such a marriage produces illumination and joy, and a fusion of consciousness. Shakespeare's allegorical poem, *The Phoenix and Turtle*, illustrates the same mystical union of love.

Modern archaeological, historical and architectural research has determined that the circular yard of The Globe theatre was delineated by a 70 ft diameter circle, around which the galleries were placed, whilst the square yard of The Fortune theatre was set out as a 55 x 55 ft square. A square of 55 x 55 ft will 'square' a circle of 70 ft diameter, as the circumference of the circle and the perimeter of the square each measure 220 ft.

The research further determined that the design of The Globe theatre was most probably derived from the traditional methods referred to as '*ad quadratum*' and '*ad triangulum*', well known to master craftsmen, and laid out using traditional measuring instruments which, when used in this geometric fashion, automatically give the correct measures for a temple or 'microcosm' of the world and universe. The full geometry consists of squares within circles within squares. In sacred or so-called Vitruvian architecture, the largest square containing everything else measures 10 x 10 units (or in this instance, 100 x 100 ft). This represents the Macrocosm, relating to the cipher 10 which signifies the All. The (largest) circle contained within this Macrocosm Square contains a second square of approximately 7 x 7 units (or 70 x 70 ft). This second square signifies the Microcosm. The 10 unit (100 ft) diameter circle contained within the Macrocosm and containing the Microcosm is the metaphorical link between the two. The Microcosm Square then contains within itself a series of lesser microcosms, all similarly linked and related mathematically. For instance, the circle inside the second square contains a third square of 5 x 5 units (or 50 x 50 ft), and the circle inside this third square contains a fourth square of approx. 3.5 x 3.5 units (or 35 x 35 ft).

The second square (70 x 70 ft) and its containing circle (100 ft diameter) delineate the outermost dimensions of The Globe theatre. The third square (50 x 50 ft) and its containing circle (70 ft diameter) determine the ground plan of The Globe theatre's yard – the area that is open to the sky within the surrounding superstructure of covered galleries. In this way The Globe theatre represents the Cosmic Globe, the Microcosm within and linked to the Macrocosm, as well as the microcosm that is our world, all in a harmony of proportion and relationship.

Within The Globe theatre, as in any structure designed according to sacred principles, there is a definite chakra system. In fact, there are several chakra systems, all of which are harmonically related and important to the use and magical effect of the theatre. Consciously or unconsciously, both actors and audiences are affected by these. With the help of diagrams from Cesariano's edition of Vitruvius, it is possible to perceive how various parts of the theatre relate to the different chakras and parts of the human body, just as in all well-designed temple and church architecture.

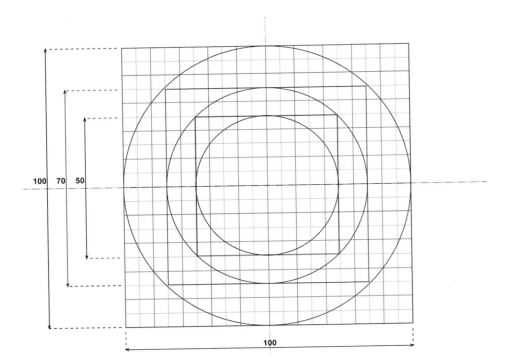

The outer square represents the Macrocosm, the middle square the Microcosm and the inner square a form of lesser microcosm

Macrocosmic Man

Using Vitruvius' 10 x 10 Square of the Macrocosm, the figure of Macrocosmic Man can be seen lying embodied in the ground-plan of The Globe in such a way that the crown of his head and soles of his feet touch the perimeter of the building at the south-west (the tiring house) and north-east points respectively. His root chakra and generative organ at the base of his spine marks the centre of the whole theatre. Whilst his thighs, knees and calves are contained in the yard of the theatre, his main body with its chakra system is associated with and represented architecturally by the stage and tiring house. The *frons scaenæ* passes across the chest of Macrocosmic Man such that the theatre's 'discovery place' with its 'royal portal' (the central door in the *frons scaenæ*) marks the heart chakra of this spiritual archetype.

In this scenario, all the acting on stage takes place 'below' the horizon of the heart, in the lower chakras of Macrocosmic Man. The higher chakras of the upper chest, shoulders, neck and head of the Macrocosmic Man lie behind the *frons scaenæ*, concealed in the actor's tiring house. It

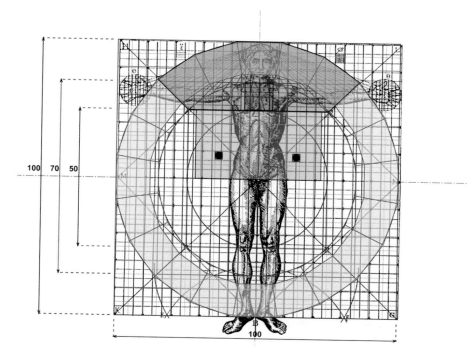

Macrocosmic Man and its relation to the Globe Theatre design

is from this inner 'higher' region, signifying heaven, that all the actors don their costumes or 'attire' and come to play their roles in the outer 'lower' region, the stage of the world. It is also the locality to which they return after they have played their roles. All this is in imitation of life.

Microcosmic Man

Using Vitruvius' 7 x 7 Square of the Microcosm, the figure of Microcosmic Man can be seen lying spread-eagled saltire-wise within The Globe theatre, with the tips of his fingers and toes touching the 10-unit diameter circle and corners of the 7 x 7 square. In the way the theatre is orientated, these corners mark the main directions of north, south, east and west. The whole body of Microcosmic Man lies stage-side of the *frons scaenæ*, in public view, with his sacral chakra marking the centre of the theatre, his heart positioned centre stage, and the crown of his head located in the 'royal portal' and 'discovery place'. In this way, the crown of Microcosmic

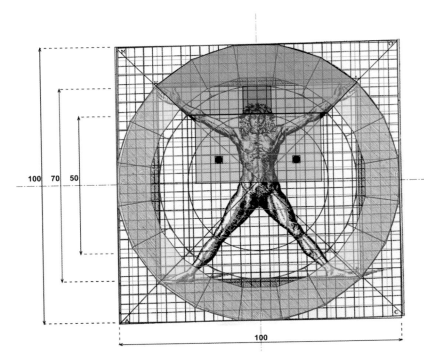

Microcosmic Man relates to the cardinal directions of the Globe Theatre design

Man lies on the heart of Macrocosmic Man – a secret that is also conveyed in the Mystery of the Last Supper wherein the beloved disciple John lays his head on the breast of Christ.

An alternative arrangement of Microcosmic Man was drawn by Henry Cornelius Agrippa, in which Microcosmic Man is associated with a pentagram set within the 7-unit (or 70 ft) diameter circle of the Microcosm. In Agrippa's arrangement, the whole head of Microcosmic Man lies in the discovery place, the solar plexus chakra (represented in Agrippa's diagram by the sun symbol) is located centre stage, and the root chakra and male generative organ (represented in Agrippa's drawing by the moon) marks the centre of the theatre. The pentagram is a traditional symbol for the human being, as the structure of the human body is based upon pentagonal geometry. The rose, which is also governed by pentagonal geometry, is another symbol of the human being. Since The Globe has twenty bays of galleries that form the enclosing circle of the theatre, this design encapsulates the Rosicrucian idea of the rose blooming on the cross (i.e. 5 and 4, wherein 5 x 4 = 20).

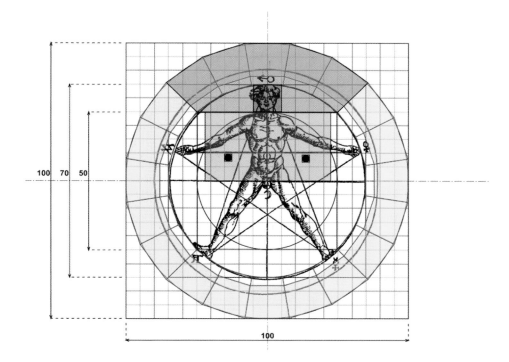

Agrippa's Microcosmic Man is associated with the pentagon, a traditional symbol of the human being

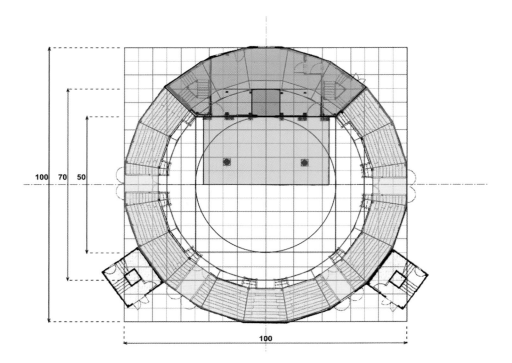

The twenty bays of the theatre carry the mystery of the Rosy Cross

The Great Pillars

One of the most dramatic architectural features of The Globe theatre, from the actors' and audiences' point of view, is the pair of Great Pillars set up on the stage and supporting the heavens. These have always been important in sacred theatre design, as also in temples, and express a fundamental teaching of the Mysteries. They represent polarity, without which nothing would exist. They are commonly known as the Pillars of Hercules, but are also referred to as the Pillars of Enoch.

In legend, Enoch is commanded by God to hold heaven and earth apart. For a temporary period of time, Hercules takes over the burden. The twin pillars are representative of them holding heaven and earth apart. Sometimes the two are depicted as brothers, Enoch being the elder and wiser, and Hercules the younger and stronger. At other times they are depicted as the immortal and mortal, or sage and hero. They in fact represent Wisdom and Strength respectively, Strength being a description of what is otherwise called Intelligence in Kabala. In Mystery Schools such as Freemasonry, it is explained that Wisdom designs and Strength supports. The pillars also represent the right hand of Mercy and left hand of Judgement, the next level of manifestation of divine Wisdom and Intelligence, or heart and mind, desire and thought, force and form, light and dark.

The Ancient Greeks referred to these two opposing but fundamental principles as Friendship and Strife, associating them respectively with Aphrodite (Venus) and Ares (Mars). The myth of their love affair is an allegorical explanation of what they represent, which is that by striving together in friendship, harmony (Hermione/Harmonia) and love (Eros/

The two great pillars on the reconstructed Globe Theatre stage

Cupid) are born. Harmony and Love, which is Beauty, is the name of the Middle Pillar, represented by the centre stage of the theatre upon which the central action takes place and where lovers embrace, and also by the discovery place where revelations are made. It is in the discovery place, for instance, that Hermione is revealed and brought back to life in Shakespeare's *A Winter's Tale*. In *The Tempest*, it is Prospero's cell where the lovers, Miranda and Ferdinand, are discovered playing chess – the Mystery game played on an 8 x 8 chessboard, which 'squares' the 10 diameter Cosmic Circle and is representative of the game (or play) of life.

The meaning of the Great Pillars is also contained in the myth of the Gemini, the immortal and mortal twins. The Great Pillars in fact constitute the astrological sigil of Gemini, the zodiacal sign of which rules the shoulders and arms. The Gemini are sons of Zeus and Leda, the Swan. As such they are symbolised as a pair of swans, hatched from swan eggs, but are also known as spear-shakers who, like St George, the Red or Rose Cross Knight, shake their spears of light at the dragons, which in this setting are seen as symbols of ignorance. The Gemini are used as key symbols in the Shakespeare works, appearing in the emblematic headpieces displayed prominently on each of the three main bodies of published work – the poems, sonnets and plays. In the Shakespeare Folio of plays, the Gemini appear as twin boys seated on two A's – the 'Double A' sign of the Mystery Schools that, amongst many things, signifies Aphrodite and Ares.

Ben Jonson refers to his 'beloved, The Author, Mr William Shakespeare' as 'the sweet Swan of Avon'. This has a mystery connotation and refers back to the Orphic Mysteries, wherein Orpheus, the great poet, is called the Swan, as also are all hierophants of the Orphic Mysteries thereafter. The symbolism is echoed in the Hindu Mysteries, wherein the twins Ham and Sa, through their love, become united as the Hamsa Swan, the vehicle of Brahma and Saraswati. Brahma is the divine creator via sound or Word (i.e. wisdom); Saraswati is the goddess of poetry and the arts that give form to the Word (i.e. express the wisdom). There is a great mystery teaching contained in the Swan. By means of the Swan the universe is created.

The Shakespeare Circle knew exactly what this all meant and used the knowledge accordingly – even to the extent of generating a focus in the area of Cygnus (the constellation of the Swan) in the Landscape Zodiac of Britain in which the Shakespeare plays could be performed and do their work of recreating the universe of our world. This Landscape Zodiac was recognised and its basis laid out by the Ancient Britons many centuries before the Christian era. Subsequent rulers and Mystery Schools, including the Church, have known something of it now and again. The Tudors regained the knowledge and the Rosicrucians in England used it for a time, before it was 'lost' again, but not without leaving signs and markers to assist its rediscovery.

The Cygnus area of the British Landscape Zodiac is what is now termed 'the Shakespeare Country', wherein lies Stratford-upon-Avon. The centre of this Zodiac is marked by High Cross, the ancient centre of Celtic and

The British Landscape Zodiac centred on the crossing of the Fosse Way and Watling Street at High Cross in Leicestershire

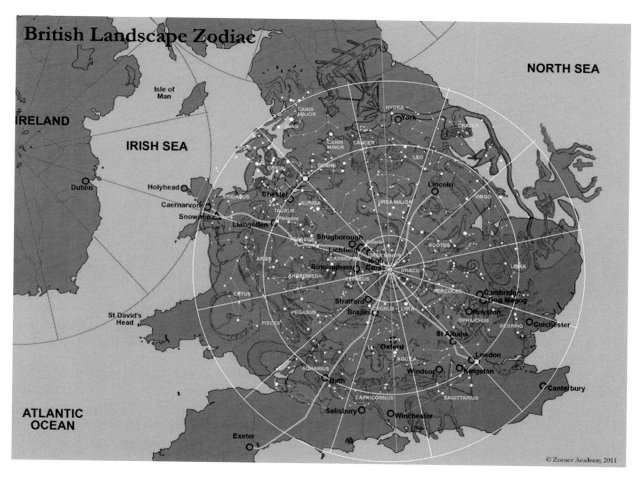

The visionary statue, The Dream, is sited on the Gemini-Taurus cusp of the British Landscape Zodiac

Roman Britain where Watling Street (now the A5 main road) crosses the Fosse Way. The zodiacal ecliptic passes through London, with the City and its White Tower ostensibly marking the cusp of Sagittarius-Scorpio. Remarkably, because apparently done without any knowledge of the British Landscape Zodiac, the opposite cusp of Gemini-Taurus has recently been marked by a beautiful sculpture that rises high into the sky like a huge white pillar. It is called 'The Dream'.

Sculpted by world-renowned Catalan artist Jaume Plensa and standing on an old spoil tip of the disused Sutton Manor Colliery near St Helens, The Dream is a twenty-metre-high elongated sculpture of a girl's neck and head with her eyes closed in meditation. Coated in sparkling white Spanish dolomite as a contrast to the coal which used to be mined here, it represents looking to a brighter future and the transforming of darkness into light, ugliness into beauty, pollution into purity and wasteland into park. A great symbol of hope, it is placed in exactly the right position in terms of the British Landscape Zodiac, on the cusp that acts, in combination with its opposite cusp, as the solstitial marker of the start of a new Great Age – an Age which, this time round, is prophesied to be a Golden Age.

Interestingly, in Hindu tradition a single white stone pillar or lingam is emblematic of a Golden Age, whereas black ones, which have been used in India for the past few thousand years, are symbolic of a Dark Age. Likewise, a single white pillar is the symbol of Atlas, the legendary king of Atlantis who presides over a Golden Age. The prophecies are that Atlantis is or will be rising again, as a New Atlantis, which is a metaphor for the creation of a new Golden Age.

Right now, in these years in which we are presently living (c.1980-2016), the midsummer sun is on the cusp of Gemini-Taurus in the celestial zodiac, and the midwinter sun is on the cusp of Sagittarius-Scorpio. This arrangement traditionally marks the start of a new Great Age of 26000 years. According to interpreters of the Mayan Calendar, the year 2012 – the year of the London Olympics and the Queen's Diamond Jubilee – is the key year that signals the ultimate starting moment of the new Great Age. If all goes well, it will be a Golden Age – but it is we who have to build it.

The Great Fire of London, with Ludgate and Old St Paul's Cathedral

SIR CHRISTOPHER WREN'S SECRET LONDON

Anthony Thorley

It was on August 27th 1666 that a party of officials could be seen walking under the transept of St Paul's, the great medieval cathedral of London. Among their number, and by no means the most senior, was a young astronomer architect from Oxford, thirty-nine-year-old Dr Christopher Wren. For some months Dr Wren had been studying the decaying fabric and dangerous stresses which threatened to make the old cathedral unsafe for worship. Now he was part of a group appointed by the king, Charles II, to make recommendations to secure its future. In his report Dr Wren made suggestions for a series of radical changes but within eight days his proposals were made redundant, as the cathedral church had been reduced to a charred ruin by the Great Fire of London.

The Great Fire of 1666

After the Great Plague of 1665, the Great Fire was the second of two disasters visited upon England's capital city within two years. Remarkably, these dire events had been predicted by the respected Commonwealth astrologer, William Lilly, as early as 1648, and further specific portents of doom had been indicated by the eclipses of the sun and moon seen over London in June 1666. At the time, superstition abounded about these matters and so following the disastrous Plague of 1665 which claimed the lives of tens of thousands of Londoners right into the spring of the following year, the population had barely recovered through the summer of 1666 before the Great Fire struck them down again. Originating in a baker's shop in Pudding Lane just north of London Bridge in the early hours of September 2nd and driven by an unusually stiff easterly wind, the fire devastated two-thirds of the City of London before finally burning itself out three days later. Although the death toll was very low – as most people were able to flee the flames in safety – tens of thousands of citizens were made homeless, camping out in the fields and open spaces outside the burned area. London would never be the same again.

Before the Great Fire, London was a warren of narrow streets and lanes lined by mainly wood and wattle houses, whose upper storeys were often only a few feet apart. The streets were littered with unhealthy rubbish, fresh water was often far from the houses and drainage commonly little more than an open sewer. It was a recipe for disease and a profoundly serious fire risk. The diarist John Evelyn, widely-travelled adviser to King Charles, was trying to interest the King and the City of London in schemes to widen the streets and improve the pavements long before disaster struck. Evelyn had seen the fine cities of continental Europe and knew how far behind lagged the unchanged medieval template of London. He also knew Wren personally and it is likely that both men were concerned about improving the city, even to the extent of drawing up radical new street plans in the years before the Great Fire. Known personally to the King since his childhood, Wren had been asked by Charles II in 1665 to make a special visit to Paris to meet with architects and study the buildings and planning of that most advanced city and return with inspiration and proposals. Wren was actually in France for much of the time the Plague raged, and although little detail is known of the work he did whilst there, it is certain that his experience in France greatly influenced his subsequent ideas for a re-planned London.

John Evelyn's plan for London after the Great Fire

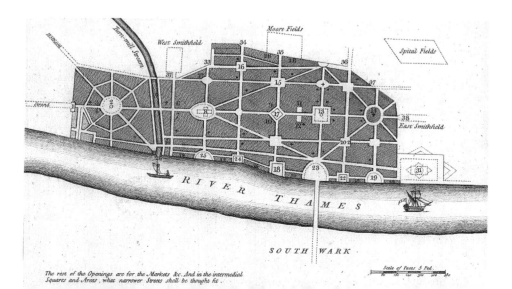

The rest of the Openings are for the Markets &c. And in the intermedial Squares and Areas, what narrower Streets shall be thought fit.

Wren takes his Plan to the King

It appears likely that Wren was resident in London as the Fire swept through the city, because within a few days he was able to make a crude map of the destroyed area and begin to draft out a new street plan. A number of gifted individuals, including John Evelyn and the uniquely talented scientist Robert Hooke, also saw the destruction of the city as an opportunity for a completely new London to be rebuilt out of the ashes. Evelyn's plan, the first of three versions, was personally presented to King Charles as early as September 13th. It is said that the King remarked on its similarity to Wren's plan, which he had seen only two days before.

For Wren to produce a basic plan of such radical and complex form within a week of the end of the fire seems unlikely. It is more probable that key features of the plan had been in his mind for some time, at least since returning from France in March that year, and that he may well have been in regular discussion with Evelyn about the basic template of a new modern London which could rival the great cities of Europe. The King is said to have been enthusiastic about Wren's radical design as it fitted in with understandable ambitions of both the King and his supporters – following the King's recent return to the monarchy after the long interregnum – to

Wren's radical plan for a new city of London from a print of 1744. The area devastated by the Fire is shown with a darker background.

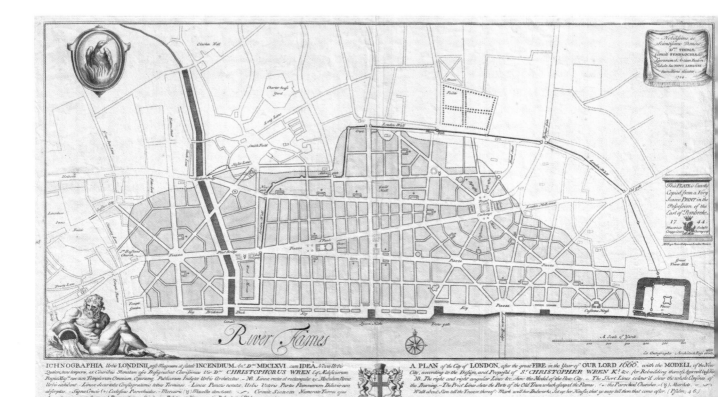

herald the dawning of a golden age of planning development, trade and culture. What better for the new King than to have a brand new city? But from the outset, there were problems in realising Wren's ambitious ideas. Almost all the streets, piazzas and key buildings, such as the new Royal Exchange and the new churches as Wren envisaged them, were occupying brand new sites on the plan, and to clear the way for such a redevelopment would require months of legal negotiation and likely expensive compensation for existing landowners.

Although enthused by the plan, it is possible that the King, remembering the execution of his father in 1649 for maintaining his divine right to power, had no appetite for the inevitable personal unpopularity that would result from trying to drive through such a radical redevelopment. Also, the traders and merchants of the city were keen to return to business as soon as possible, for London as a trading city depended on commerce for its lifeblood. It is said that Parliament favoured Robert Hooke's more basic plan of a series of regular blocks, but in the event none of these new schemes ever saw the light of day and apart from a little street-widening, the development of the River Fleet as a trading waterway and the introduction of obligatory use of more fire-resistant stone and brick for all new house building, the city was essentially redeveloped on the old pre-fire street plan. Remarkably, the bulk of the rebuilding of the city was completed in just four years.

Wren's Early Scheme for Nineteen Churches

In early October 1666, King Charles appointed Wren to the Rebuilding Commission, a small committee set up to advise him as to the best way to rebuild London. Within weeks of starting this work, Wren must have realised that the practical likelihood of his own ambitious plan being taken up was very slight, yet there is early evidence from this time that Wren did not simply shelve the plan as a failed ambition but from the outset sought to conserve some of its key features. To understand why this might have been requires us to examine the basis of his plan in a little more detail.

Wren's plan centres on a series of piazzas and wide boulevards

classical tradition and like many emerging scientists at the birth of that period we now call the Enlightenment, he would have no intellectual problem reconciling his scientific and rational self with more symbolic and traditional insights without ever slipping into accusations of superstition or magical thinking.

It can be easily seen how Wren divided his cityscape into recognisable geometric figures. If we start with the obvious octagon west of the River Fleet (an octagonal scheme incidentally shared in common with John Evelyn), we can pass eastwards over the Fleet and up Ludgate Hill to St Paul's. It can be seen that the Cathedral is at the centre of a grid of parallel streets that make up a square. This abuts on a pentagonal figure which sits next to a hexagon. Within the hexagon are seven-sided and nine-sided figures, the heptagon and the nonagon. Right in the centre of Wren's proposed Royal Exchange area is a piazza with ten sides and ten street entrances, a decagon. Between London Bridge, Aldgate and a point on the great boulevard is a classic right-angled Pythagorean triangle, with sides of 3, 4 and 5 units.

Of course none of these numerical geometric figures or their potential symbolism and deeper meaning of number ever saw the light of day, and yet it appears that in his design and choice of existing church sites and their reconstruction, Wren did his best to encapsulate and represent their essential features. The historical details and full narrative of this remarkable pattern of reconstruction and encryption form the basis of a much more detailed account than can be represented here, and so only a brief outline will be given. The fifty-one churches to be rebuilt can be seen as more or less randomly placed on the map of the burned area of the city. Although many are close together, their wide distribution across the burned area offered Wren the possibility of choosing church sites very close to original features of his master plan such as piazzas and boulevards. By choosing churches in this way Wren was able to conserve, albeit cryptically, the main features of both his geometric numerical figures and the basic triangular scheme of the dividers.

Take the octagon west of the Fleet. Wren locates a church site just east of its central piazza. This is the site of the reconstructed St Bride's Church.

The western octagon showing the position of St Bride Fleet Street

The octagonal tiered spire of St Bride Fleet Street

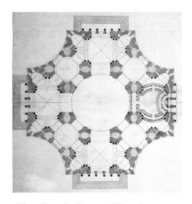

The Greek Cross, Wren's favoured first design for St Paul's Cathedral

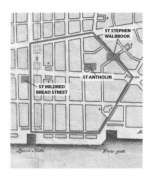

*Pentagon showing
positions of pentagonal
St Antholin, St Mildred
Bread Street and
St Stephen Walbrook*

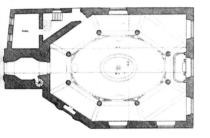

*The pentagonal plan of
St Antholin church*

*Hexagon showing
positions of hexagonal
St Olave Jewry and
St Stephen Walbrook
on the pentagon/
hexagon interface*

The final steeple design of that church is a spectacular series of octagonal tiers (giving rise incidentally to the design of the traditional wedding cake) rising to over two hundred feet, perhaps the most famous octagonal shape in all British architecture. So the principle of the octagon is thus enshrined within the virtual octagon of Wren's original plan. Moving eastwards to the figure of the square, we find St Paul's Cathedral exactly in its centre. Wren's early plan for the new Cathedral, and one he tended personally to favour, was based on an equi-armed Greek Cross, an exact square plan. So in its original conception, St Paul's was to be four-square within a much larger virtual square of spacious new streets. It is perhaps no coincidence that the principal church of the city representing heaven above is placed on the square, as the geometric form of the square is traditionally the symbol for the earth below.

On the boundary of the square and the pentagon is a road known as Bread Street. The church chosen by Wren as lying on the boundary of his four-sided and five-sided figures is known as St Mildred Bread Street. Uniquely for a Wren design, this church has four main windows in the body of the church and five false windows facing the street, an ingenious combination of four and five. Close to the centre of the virtual pentagon is the church of St Antholin. In order to allow for a street-widening scheme (or so the conventional explanation goes), Wren had to modify the shape of this church rebuild, and so it ended up having a five-sided shape. It was also actually five-sided in its original internal design until an additional inner wall rearranged its internal symmetry into a more balanced six-sided form. In this way, Wren created a five-sided church in the centre of his pentagonal figure.

The prediction you may now feel inclined to make is that within the next of his figures, the hexagon, there has to be a six-sided church. Such a church cannot be found in the actual centre of the hexagon, as the hexagon nests the heptagon, nonagon and decagon, but a six-sided church is found on the boundary of the hexagon. This is St Olave Jewry. Its six-sided form is aesthetically most subtle, and owes nothing to limitations of the actual building site. The only explanation for its shape is that Wren chose the six-sidedness as part of his design and by so doing was pointing up the virtual hexagon.

On the interface of the pentagon and the hexagon figures is the great Wren church, St Stephen Walbrook. Following the example of the interface church St Mildred Bread Street, we might expect to find the encryption of the numbers five and six in the basic window design. And so we do. On the north and south walls of St Stephen's there are six window bays and on the east side there are five, a simple ploy of design which emphasises the five/six interface. Further churches within the nested heptagon and nonagon encrypt the numbers seven and nine, and finally we identify perhaps Wren's most remarkable burned church site, fortunately for him located right in the centre of his virtual ten-sided piazza figure at the core of his proposed financial centre. This is St Benet Fink, noted by many architectural historians as being unique and something of a mystery in having ten sides: a decagonal church we can now see to be logically placed according to Wren's scheme within a virtual decagon! Note also how its six central pillars may be taken to represent the centre of the hexagon figure so enabling the church to combine hexagonal and decagonal features.

Another St Benet church, in Gracechurch Street, provides the geometry to represent the 3,4,5 Pythagorean triangle. Thus Wren has encapsulated all the numbers and geometric forms between three and ten in the form of encrypted churches and so conserved the vision of his harmonious universe in the newly emerging city. I hear the curious reader enquiring what of numbers one and two? One has to be an isolated point in the landscape and is almost certainly the Monument to the Fire, in Fish Street, designed with Robert Hooke and erected on a church site some two hundred and two feet from the baker's shop in Pudding Lane. The Monument carries its own powerful symbolism of endurance and survival. The number two is simply a line between two places, and where that is located might have to remain a mystery!

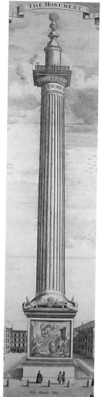

The Monument to the Fire of London, finished in 1677. From a print of 1753

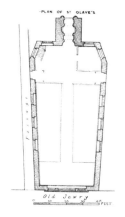

The hexagonal plan of St Olave Jewry

Inner decagon showing Wren's new Royal Exchange and the position of St Benet Fink church

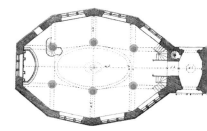

Decagonal plan of St Benet Fink with an internal hexagon of pillars

The eastern octagon and piazza showing positions of St Margaret Pattens (octagonal spire) and St Mary at Hill (domed)

St Margaret Pattens

Wren's possible London Stone Piazza. Both St Mary Abchurch and St Swithin London Stone positioned close to the proposed piazza are domed churches.

The Domed Churches

Wren did not stop there. He seemed also determined to demarcate the several notable piazzas that join the geometric figures together and produce the sunburst of roads that come off London Bridge. The key cryptic indicator to the piazza positions seems to have been Wren's use of domed churches. Wren only designed seven churches with domes that were actually completed, and each one fulfils a special role or place in the jigsaw puzzle of his city plan. The great piazza of St Paul's is clearly graced by the finest dome in Wren's total architectural output, but St Mildred on Bread Street is also domed, as is St Antholin in the centre of the pentagon. St Stephen Walbrook, the other interface church, is also domed, as is St Benet Fink sitting in the centre of the hexagon, heptagon, nonagon and decagon.

There are three other striking piazzas. One is the eastern octagon marked by two churches: St Margaret Pattens, a unique octagonal spire some two hundred feet high, perhaps a balance for the octagonal steeple of St Bride's, and close by, St Mary at Hill, with its unique dome. The church Wren chose to place on his sunburst piazza at the north end of London Bridge is St Magnus the Great. It has a domed steeple, as did St Benet Gracechurch Street, the church Wren chose to represent his triangle figure. The other piazza area, with six street entrances, is marked by two domed churches close by each other: St Mary Abchurch and St Swithin London Stone. Wren recognised the importance of the London Stone to London's symbolic and mythic history, and may have been planning to locate it in the centre of his planned piazza. As no piazza was possible, he had it placed by the wall of his St Swithin church design. Hence each piazza or meeting place of key roads as well as the centre of each geometric figure was marked by a domed church, the dome being another symbol of the heavenly vault or the universe in harmony.

The Eclipse Predictor

Finally, returning to Wren's attempt to encrypt his dividers, we can identify his most radical and bold symbolic plan. The original dividers on his city street plan reveal two sides of another Pythagorean triangle, this time displaying proportions of 5, 12, and 13. The twelve-unit side is found between Ludgate and the relocated Royal Exchange decagon and the five-unit side is between the decagon and the sunburst piazza by London Bridge. The remaining thirteen-unit side would be an alignment between the sunburst piazza and Ludgate, but is not marked. Why is this? In Wren's scheme, the key feature is to create the geometric formula of transecting the five-unit side at the point three units from the right angle, thus making a unique triangle with an angle at Ludgate of fourteen degrees. This slim triangle, immediately recognisable as the basis of the dividers, enables a length to be calculated from Ludgate along the south-eastern boulevard which can be used to represent a period of time and so enable the prediction of eclipses of the sun and moon. The thirteen-unit side or alignment is not required for this geometric calculation and hence Wren did not include it in his original plan.

Eclipses occur about every one hundred and seventy-three days so that the Eclipse Year is represented by three hundred and forty-six days. This number of days set out as a measure of distance can be represented at three key points along the boulevard. As a skilful astronomer and mathematician known to be preoccupied with eclipse prediction, Wren indicated the most prominent position for eclipse prediction on his plan. It is exactly where the wide north-south boulevard between Queens Hythe Dock and Cripplegate crosses the south-east boulevard which commences at Ludgate. Here, Wren

Wren's 5,12,13 triangle system can be used to predict eclipses. St Clement Eastcheap is positioned at the 3:2 point and St Mildred Bread Street is the closest church to the geographical eclipse point.

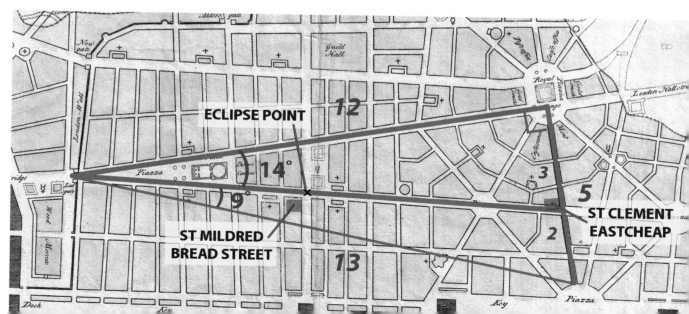

placed a square market-place piazza and two adjoining churches on his original plan, as if to further emphasise this crucial eclipse- prediction place in the cityscape. Perhaps he envisaged the east-west boulevard as some form of processional way which would ceremonially revisit this eclipse point and so, through conscious knowledge of eclipses, astronomical or metaphorical, enable the population of London to avoid great disasters such as the Plague and the Fire in the future. However, denied the existence of the boulevard and the crossing point, he once again had to use two city churches to encapsulate the eclipse phenomenon: St Clement Eastcheap, and that other most important church, St Mildred Bread Street, the closest actual church to the crossing point and place of eclipse prediction.

Once again, Wren had secured a symbolic protective design, a kind of architectural amulet in the form of the dividers, by utilising the positions of rebuilt churches and building into their design the cryptic numerical features which represented the original plan. The dividers were the bare bones of a sophisticated mathematical model for eclipse prediction. Eclipses were still seen as portents of disaster in Wren's time and had been invoked in predicting the Plague and the Great Fire. We are led to presume that everything Wren integrated into his city plan was aimed at decreasing the likelihood of any further disasters eclipsing or part-eclipsing the future of London. By building into his design an eclipse predictor, he was enabling the city to be better prepared for any future disasters. In this remarkable way, Wren integrated a powerful series of geometric and mathematical forms across the city like protective amulets: a series of geometric shapes between one and ten representing the harmonious universe, domed churches in key positions envisaging the heavenly vault overseeing the city's fortunes and a vast eclipse predictor to better prepare the city against future catas-trophe. In this process, Wren was unaffectedly exercising his intellectual skills as a rational scientist with his understanding of traditional symbolic form arising out of classical teaching.

With hindsight we could say that Wren was actively strengthening an already sacred landscape into a more secure form, creating a cryptic energetic template which would protect London in its long history and future. Has he succeeded? Many of his special churches have been pulled

down, demolished or destroyed in redevelopment and the drama of two
World Wars, and yet Wren's basic protective pattern clearly endures into
the twenty-first century and continues to make London one of the most
vibrant, successful and richly rewarding cities in the world.

*St Paul's Cathedral
became a protective
icon in the bombing of
the Second World War.
The spire is of another
Wren church, St Martin's
on Ludgate Hill.*

EAST

Reduced from seventeen six inches to one mile
O.S. Sheets, in order to fit Philips' Planisphere

WEST

Reproduced from the Ordnance Survey Map with the
sanction of the Controller of H.M. Stationery Office

The Zodiacal Giants of Somerset correspond with the Stars of their respective
Celestial Constellations.

*Maltwood's 1935
Glastonbury Zodiac*

*Katharine Maltwood
in 1905*

GALACTIC HEART:
LONDON AND
THE BRITISH LANDSCAPE ZODIAC

Anthony Thorley

Imagine the heavenly circle of twelve constellations through which the sun appears to pass on its yearly round. Now literally drop them out of the sky and set the stars framing the traditional effigies of the zodiac, such as lion, bull and virgin, on the landscape and see in your mind's eye a shimmering circle some thirty miles round and eleven miles across. There you have the Glastonbury Zodiac, nested in the countryside of Somerset in the south-west of England. This most visionary phenomenon, literally joining heaven and earth, was first recognised by a remarkable mystic, artist and student of the esoteric, Katharine Emma Maltwood (1878-1961), whilst resident near Glastonbury around 1917.

Maltwood did not immediately recognise the animal effigies as zodiacal, however. She had been reading of the knights' tales in an Arthurian romance, *The High History of the Holy Graal*, allegedly written by the monks of Glastonbury Abbey in the early thirteenth century, when she began to see that the knights' adventures with maidens, giants and lions were identifiably taking place in the Somerset countryside around Glastonbury Abbey.

In a profound personal epiphany, she first discovered the figure of a lion around the royal town of Somerton, etched in the line of the River Cary, the woodlands composing its mane and the front paw stamping its authority on the town. She quickly made a sketch of its convincing outline. Soon after, she identified the earthly form of a giant a little to the north of Dundon (now recognised as one of the twins of Gemini) and went on to see the beginnings of other figures emerging from the land – all of them consistent with the Arthurian stories. Then, the story goes, a London friend visited

Katharine and suggested that the figures she had discovered might more probably form one of the zodiacs on the land proposed in the 1880s by the co-founder of the Theosophical Society, Madame Blavatsky. At the time, Blavatsky did not identify exactly where on the earth such zodiacs might be located, but she did propose the idea of the actual physical existence of landscape zodiacs. Maltwood soon realised that this was indeed a zodiac on the ground, but a zodiac also uniquely incorporating the legends and stories of the Arthurian epic. In the years immediately after the Great War of 1914-18, she consolidated her findings to identify all twelve zodiacal effigies. She additionally discovered a thirteenth figure, a great guardian dog (an ancient symbol of English sovereignty) near Langport town: a dog, in the place of the constellation of Canis Major, literally guarding the heavenly circle.

For the rest of her life and long after she had emigrated to Canada in 1938, Maltwood tirelessly researched the Glastonbury Zodiac, realising that each effigy carried its own folklore, myths, legends, place-names and local history in a way that went far beyond a simple Arthurian context. This research confronted her with such a convincing body of evidence in, for example, the synchronicity of zodiacally significant place-names (for example, the Guardian Dog's tail is at Wagg and its ear at Earlake) that she was convinced that the Zodiac had been constructed some four thousand years ago by Sumerian priest-engineers who had sailed from *Sum*-eria to found *Sum*-erset!

Katharine Maltwood's fanciful archaeology is now easily dismissed, as indeed is the whole concept of the Zodiac, as nothing but the passionate projection or virtual invention of an eccentric artist-millionairess with time on her hands, but for those of us who have followed in her footsteps as students of the Zodiac (and indeed of other zodiacs, for there are over forty now identified in England alone!), the effigies in the landscape confront us with a profound set of phenomena and experiences which really challenge our ideas about linear time and simple cause and effect. Fascinatingly, there is no explicit reference to the Glastonbury Zodiac as existing or being recognised in any of the historical records about Somerset county before Maltwood's own visionary moment as the lion of Leo blazed through her

Maltwood's outline of the Lion in Somerset

Bartholomew map into her consciousness. The same is true for all the other zodiacs discovered in Britain. They are all modern discoveries and in the historical record do not predate the initial perception of their discoverers. And yet there is overwhelming evidence that in these modern zodiacs, the landscape has slowly shaped itself over the centuries in changing field boundaries, road outlines, drainage ditches and patterns of human occupation to produce, by the early twentieth century (but not before), identifiable zodiacal effigies. There are many examples where formless landscape of hundreds of years ago has over the decades slowly taken up the form of the effigy, incorporated the synchronicities of legend, history and place-names associated with the specific zodiacal sign, so producing a kind of drift into contemporary perceptual clarity.

My own research into this matter suggests that the zodiac landscape seems to call its discoverers, to pull them into the discovering process so that they come to have a profound sense of dialogue between land and person. It is as if the land speaks. So often I have been told: 'I didn't discover the zodiac on the land, it discovered me!' But how can this be? Such a process of complex interaction and natural historical development without any evidence of human contrivance or an overlying master-plan cannot be simply explained as the mere psychological projection or fanciful invention of one person. So how do we begin to explain it?

The Gypsy Switch

One person who was apparently pulled into a zodiacal adventure of her own was Jill Smith in the early 1980s. Well acquainted with the mythology of the Glastonbury Zodiac, she had walked its effigies on many occasions. As a painter, poet and performing artist she had a particular sensitivity to the land and its rich imagery. One day, in a Glastonbury café, she was given a map of a gypsy journey around England by an old travelling man. He explained that this journey was called the Gypsy Switch (switch possibly being a reference to the switch or whip which the gypsies used to encourage the horses pulling their caravans) and that it had died out as a traditional annual circuit in the 1920s. The map divided England into twelve sections,

Jill Smith's map of the Gypsy Switch

each one being a sign of the zodiac, and in the space of one year, the travelling gypsies moved through all the signs of the zodiac on the map, spending a month in each sign at the appropriate zodiacal time of the year, before moving on the next one. Many of the places they visited apparently had horse fairs, such as the famous Appleby Fair in Cumbria (the Gemini section), and all were in England except for the sign of Taurus, which involved a journey across the Irish Sea to the horse fairs in Ireland. In the centre of this circle of zodiacal places is the beautiful recumbent stone circle in Derbyshire known as Arbor Low.

Utterly intrigued by this old tradition, Jill Smith decided to carry out the journey round the year in her own horse-drawn trailer. Over two years, sometimes accompanied by friends, sometimes simply on foot carrying her baby son Taliesin, she completed the entire circuit and wrote up her account as a series of poems in a self-published booklet in 1985. The following year, I heard her giving a talk about her experiences of the Switch and subsequently wrote to her to learn more of the tradition. In my later research into the Gypsy Switch circuit, it quickly became apparent to me that many of the twelve zodiacal centres were places known to have individual landscape zodiacs of their own. I already knew of landscape zodiacs described at Stonehenge, Glastonbury, Lampeter, Anglesey, Ireland, Appleby, Durham, Lincoln, Cambridge, Ongar in Essex and at Kingston on Thames in West London, making the Gypsy Switch apparently a zodiac of zodiacs. I was also aware that most of these individual zodiacs had been initially described or published without any reference to the Gypsy Switch material revealed by Jill Smith in the 1980s, making this whole national zodiacal phenomenon truly a modern earth mystery.

Over the last twenty years and quite independently of the Gypsy Switch circuit, Peter Dawkins has researched and explored a huge British Landscape Zodiac which covers the south part of England (see page 73). I found his British Zodiac equally intriguing because the basic sign positions of the circle of effigies and images tallied closely with the basic positions of the Gypsy Switch Zodiac, seeming to suggest that to sensitive explorers the landscape was revealing its secrets in a consistent way.

The Astronomical Background

It is not possible to contemplate the circle of the constellations in our northern hemisphere which make up the signs of the zodiac without considering a little basic astronomy. Each year, as seen from our standpoint on Earth, the Sun appears to traverse the zodiacal constellations, remaining in each one for just over thirty days. This annual circuit of the heavens is called the Sun's ecliptic and is only apparent, for in truth the Sun remains in the centre of our solar system and it is the annual circuit of the Earth around the relatively fixed star that is our Sun which gives us the perception of the Sun moving against the fixed stars of the constellations. For centuries, the regularity and certainty of this annual cycle have been key features in our history and cultural development, especially in developing some of the basic features of our solar calendar year.

However, if there was security and comforting predictability in the annual circuit of the Sun in the heavens, the perceptibly changing position of the sunrise at the spring equinox over hundreds of years was culturally problematic. This is because the axis of the Earth is spinning round like a giant wobbling spinning-top and very slowly, over 26000 years, traces out another circle in the sky, completely independent of the daily spin of the Earth's own axis. Over the years this means that the rising position of the Sun on the horizon slowly moves backwards against the fixed stars of the sky beyond. For at least the last two thousand years, ancient cultures were aware of this so-called precession of the Sun, which must have been confronting since it suggested that somehow the Sun and the fixed stars were not in complete synchrony and celestial harmony.

Around 4300 BCE, ancient observers watching the position of the Sun against the background constellations at the Spring Equinox (our March 21st) would see it rising against the stars of Taurus, and then between 2300 and 150 BCE against the stars of Aries. The spring sunrise takes about 2160 years to traverse each sign, and modern-day astrology has put considerable import into the idea that for two thousand years the Sun rose in the Age of Taurus, during which time the bull was worshipped and other Taurean characteristics were to the fore. Then in the two thousand years before the Common Era, the Sun went through the Age of Aries, the ram, and in dominant ancient cultures such as Ancient Egypt, the ram was a principal god of worship and Arian features were in evidence. It was around 150 BCE that the sun entered the Age of Pisces, where for the last two thousand years the fishes have been associated symbolically with the doctrine of Christianity and its controversial contribution to world culture. There is actually only slim evidence that ancient cultures and civilisations had a clear sense of these past astrological ages in their own times, but they are certainly a lively part of our own contemporary mythological thinking!

Now, at the beginning of the twenty-first century, the process of precession finds us on the cusp of the next constellation entered each year by the spring equinox sunrise: Aquarius, an astrological sign associated with science, technology and radical new thinking. For some, we have already entered that era, but relying on strict astronomy we are not quite into Aquarius, although culturally we are certainly anticipating its effects.

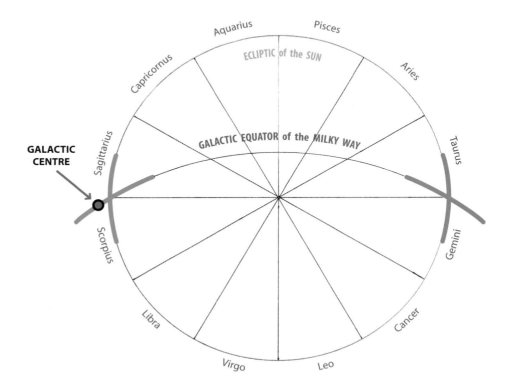

Schematic diagram of the sun's ecliptic circle and the arch of the galactic equator showing the two saltire crosses as gates to heaven

The Two Gates of Heaven

Since ancient cultures had to reconcile to the slow drift of precession through the constellations and the challenge of a predominant new age every two thousand years, they looked to other signs and places in the heavens that afforded a more secure stability. The other great circle of constellations in the sky is the Milky Way, that spectacular band of stars and star clouds which seems to encircle Earth but actually represents our perception of the sky when we look into the main body and concentration of stars which make up our galaxy. The circle of the Milky Way has generated its own mythology in cultures all around the globe as its trail across the black sky of night is such a unique celestial feature.

Many cultures hold the belief that between their lives on Earth, the souls of people reside as stars in the Milky Way, seeing this jewel in the sky as a vast repository of souls awaiting return to Earth. The circle of the Milky Way crosses the Sun's circle of zodiacal constellations, the ecliptic, at an oblique angle at two points in the sky. One of them is between the constellations of Taurus and Gemini, and the other is between the opposite pair of constellations, Sagittarius and Scorpius. The ancients noted that these two crossovers of the great circles of the sky, the ecliptic and the Milky Way, never shifted like the precessing Sun on the horizon but remained forever fixed and stable. The two oblique crossovers were so important in cultural iconography that they were called 'saltire crosses'. Saltire literally means 'leap into heaven' (the Latin word *saltus* has two meanings: leap, as in dance, and also poetically, the Elysian Fields).

So an additional significance was identified with these two crossover places in the sky. They were considered to be portals, or star-gates, to the celestial Elysian Fields of heaven, accessing the myriads of star-souls in the Milky Way. These were the traditional gateways to heaven as seen in the sky, and the souls of men were considered to incarnate to Earth through the star-gate between Gemini and Taurus, and after death, return to heaven through the opposite star-gate between Sagittarius and Scorpius. Perhaps when Christ entrusted the keys of heaven to St Peter, it was the saltire star-gates he had in mind.

St Peter's saltire keys to heaven are enshrined in the Vatican coat of arms

Astronomically, if you look into the sky between Gemini and Taurus you are looking out into deep space beyond our galaxy. If you look at the sky between Sagittarius and Scorpius you are looking in the opposite direction into the centre of our galaxy where the stars are most concentrated. There must have been some ancient awareness of this most significant part of our sky, the Galactic Centre. Although no bright stars are situated at the Centre, when you look at the nearby constellations on the ecliptic, the arrow at the end of the scorpion's tail and the arrow of Sagittarius the archer both point to exactly the same place in space, which quite simply is the centre of the galaxy. Also, the only two astrological sigils with arrows are those of Sagittarius and Scorpio! It is fascinating to consider how ancient astrological traditions and knowledge seemed to be aware of the Galactic Centre when it has only become apparent to modern astronomers in the last few hundred years.

Winter Solstice at the Galactic Centre

Across time, many cultures have also particularly valued the position on the ecliptic of the rising Sun at the winter solstice. In the European tradition of the northern hemisphere, this time in the winter months is when the Sun is at its weakest but also at a crucial turning-point when it will revive and rise each day higher and higher in the sky as it moves, once again, towards summer. Therefore, the winter solstice is a symbolic time of the almost dying and then cautious revival of solar energy. Not only the people of the Mayan civilisation in Central America but also those from many other cultures calculated centuries ago that eventually the midwinter sunrise on or close to December 21st 2012, would occur between Scorpius and Sagittarius, and on the horizon would appear to be at the star-gate which is as close to the Galactic Centre in the sky as it is possible for it to be. This juxtaposition of winter rising Sun and Galactic Centre was anticipated as being auspicious because the Sun, for the first time in 26000 years, would appear at the winter solstice (its own time of cautious revival) to be in the sky at the very place from which, at least in mythical terms, it originated. That is, as it rose over the Galactic Centre, it would appear to be reborn from the place of its own original birth.

The Sun precesses, or drifts, very slowly on the horizon, moving only one degree of the 360 degrees of the circle every seventy-two years. Thus it was not until the 1990s that the midwinter sunrise began to approximate to the position of the Galactic Centre, creating a true alignment between the Centre, the Sun and Earth, and reaching its closest position at midwinter sunrise approximately in the year 2012, then slowly drifting away beyond the Centre. In terms of astrology, this alignment or apparent juxtaposition between Earth, Sun and Galactic Centre is called a conjunction, a form of heavenly marriage or union. International interest and publicity concerning this celestial event, linked to the Mayan calendar Long Count, has led to 2012 being identified by many as a highly significant year in global cultural history.

Since this solar conjunction with the midwinter solstice at the Galactic Centre appears to portend a kind of universal rebirth, many ancient cultures from all over the world have predicted that the years around 2012 are going to be times of profound cultural change on a global scale. This is not the end of the world in the sense of a catastrophic disaster but a time of profound change for all who inhabit our planet. After this period, the world and its population of all living things, and indeed much else, will

At the Winter solstice in the years around 2012 the sun appears to rise close to the Galactic Centre which is indicated by the sting of the Scorpion and the arrow of the Sagittarian archer

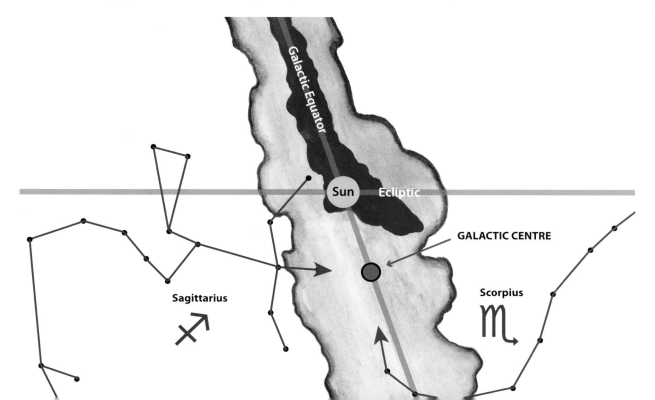

never be quite the same again. And as we contemplate the modern world, gripped at it is by social, political, environmental and financial crises which affect us all, it is clear that the ancient peoples were extraordinarily accurate in their awareness of this crucial time in global history.

The Galactic Centre on the Gipsy Switch

Aware of the implications of the Galactic Centre and its relevance to 2012, it was in 2002 that I returned to the circuit of the Gipsy Switch on the map of Britain and began to search for the place of the Galactic Centre on the map, knowing it had to be between the signs of Sagittarius and Scorpio. I knew the Sagittarius centre to be at Kingston on Thames, a place with its own landscape zodiac discovered by the late Mary Caine in the 1970s, while the Scorpio centre was at Ongar in Essex, on the north-east side of London. Again Ongar had its own landscape zodiac, described by

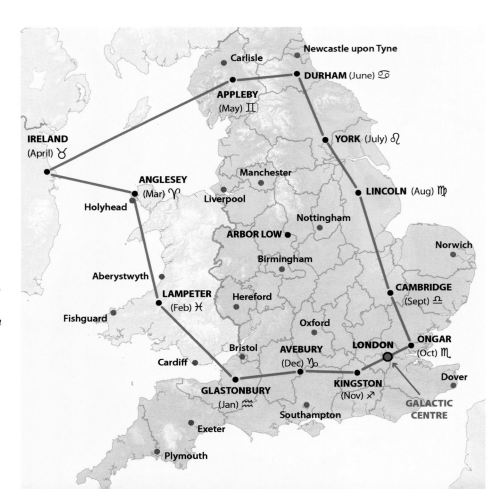

The Gypsy Switch showing the twelve zodiacal localities of the annual journey and the Galactic Centre between Scorpio and Sagittarius in East London at the site of the Olympic Games

the late Jim Kimmis in 1977. Somewhere between these two zodiacs was the place of the Galactic Centre. Well, clearly the main place between Kingston and Ongar, some thirty miles apart, was the conurbation of London, making our capital city the Galactic Centre of the Gypsy Switch Zodiac. No surprises there! But then – still in 2002 – I found that the exact midpoint between these two zodiacs was very close to Hackney in East London. This made Hackney more specifically England's Galactic Centre. As someone who had worked there, I knew Hackney to be an East End borough of London, rich in local history and part of the great working class and industrial tradition of expanding London, but not a place which suggested any particularly special geographical significance.

Another potent confirmation that London is the place of the Galactic Centre arose through the visionary work of Peter Dawkins, when he identified a vast oblique crossover, truly a saltire cross, spanning the city of London. This saltire cross was created by connecting two ancient capital cities of an earlier England, Winchester in the south-west and Colchester in the north-east, and crossing their alignment with another alignment between two ancient cities of learning and religious scholarship, Canterbury in the south-east and Oxford in the north-west. This combination of spiritual scholarship and temporal authority appropriately crossed over the city of

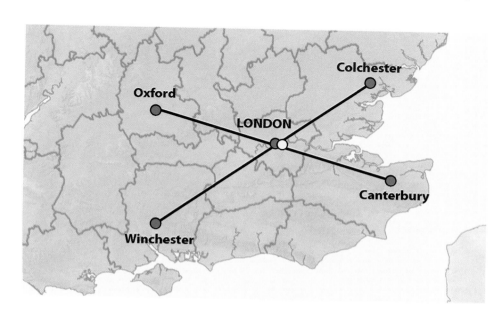

The Saltire Cross centred on London derived from four related historic cities

London, strengthening the idea that in the English landscape, London was the centre of our nation and perhaps for the lucky ones, also an entrance to heaven!

For a while, I contemplated these ides. Then around 2004, London began its preparations to mount a bid to host the Olympic Games and suddenly a huge swathe of land just beside Hackney in the lower Lea Valley had been earmarked for the main Olympic Park to host the Games. I realised that, extraordinarily, the site chosen was exactly where the Galactic Centre would be found on the Gypsy Switch circuit and that the Games would be held in the very year, 2012, when it might be expected that the cultural expectation of global renewal would be at its peak.

The thought of London hosting the 2012 Games on the Galactic Centre continued to intrigue me, but for a long while there was little realistic prospect that London would win the bid. The city of Paris was the front runner. It was well prepared with many stadia already constructed, and informed commentators saw Paris hosting the Games as a foregone conclusion. And then, the story goes, President Jacques Chirac committed an off-microphone gaffe. After a dinner, but whilst still perilously close to a live microphone, he was heard to remark that Finnish food was the worst

The Kingston on Thames Zodiac in south-west London

The Ongar Zodiac in Essex

he had ever tasted. Well, there just had to be a number of Finnish delegates on the International Olympic Committee which made the final vote. After London had been chosen by four clear votes in July 2005, one of the Finnish delegates remarked that after a comment like that from the French President, he could never have voted for Paris. How true this story is (for the curious, it is readily accessible online!) or whether it is just part of the urban myth of the London Games I am not able to say, but it strengthens my own belief that spirit moves in strange ways!

So, with the bid secured, the London Olympic Games main Olympic Park was actually going to be at the Galactic Centre of the Gypsy Switch Zodiac of zodiacs! What could be the significance of this, for the Games and for Britain in general? Play is often spoken of as the highest expression of spirit; one only has to witness the way children naturally demonstrate that pure trait. So athletes of every country in the world – representatives of the global family – have been invited by London to come to play and compete within the abiding principles of the Olympic spirit. Has the rich tradition of the English landscape enshrined in the Gypsy Switch somehow reached out and influenced the whole mysterious process of setting the Games at the Galactic Centre close by Hackney? Perhaps England called

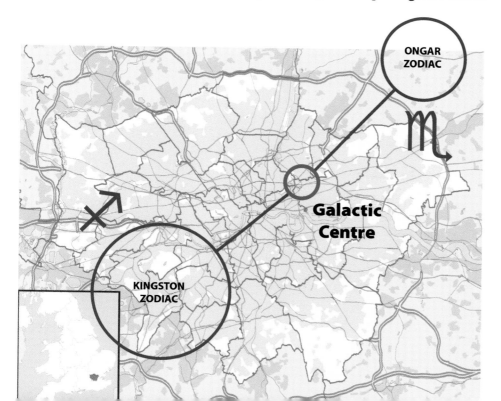

The Olympic Park as the Galactic Centre is equidistant from the centres of the Kingston and Ongar Zodiacs

together the peoples of the world in the context of the even playing-field of the Olympic Games for some higher task, as yet unknown, but somehow connected to the promise of a global renewal.

Wherever its host city, the Olympic Games' main site always carries a tradition of sacred ground. This stems from its own venerable history since the Ancient Games in Greece began and is strengthened by the ritual enactment of the opening ceremonies that surround the lighting of the Olympic Flame and the presence of a vast international audience at the stadia, which through television unites the wider world in the Olympic ideal. But the Olympic Park, most accurately at Stratford City just adjacent to Hackney, is not only conventional Olympic sacred space with all the elevation and transcendence in individual and team performances which that might generate. There is also the symbolic presence of playing on the place in the English landscape corresponding to the centre of our galaxy, and so potentially reaching into core issues which affect the whole of humanity and its future. Who can say how deeply the athletes and the spectators will be affected when in symbolic contact with such a fundamental part of our cosmology and our ultimate source? It seems inevitable that participants and spectators will return to their home countries imbued with a unique experience of the potential of the higher spirit of mankind, and possibly – hopefully – be better prepared for the profound changes still to come.

The Olympic Park at Stratford City in 2011

*Front and reverse views
of the 2012 Summer
Olympics gold medal*

The Olympic ideal revisits fundamental ideas about cooperation and fair play as well as competition, about striving individually and together. Perhaps a more balanced and harmonious world can be the promise of an Olympic Games held on the Galactic Heart.

With his winged head and flaming hair this 'Gorgon's head' carving from Roman Bath is surely a variant of the British Mercury or Lugus the Light-bearer

SACRED GAMES OF LUGH THE LIGHT-BEARER

Anthony Thorley

As the Romans proceeded to invade and conquer Europe in the years before and after the Common Era, across the entire continent they encountered the presence of a native god. Lugus, a sky-god associated in legend with the sun and the beginning of the harvest, was a very ancient god. His name first appears in southern Portugal around 700 BCE on a carved gravestone or memorial written in a now extinct Celtic language but using the script of Phoenicians who had colonies on the Mediterranean coast. Scholars believe that the widespread presence of Lugus in place-names across Europe (from Ukraine to Ireland) suggests that he might have been primarily a god of smithing and metalwork, and also one of trade and journeys. There is even a suggestion that as migrant peoples came from the eastern Mediterranean during the Bronze Age (c. 2000 BCE), bringing new ideas and possibly an early form of the Celtic language up the Atlantic seaboard to embrace Great Britain and Ireland, the cult of Lugus as a trade god was a key element.

The importance of Lugus is evidenced in the number and variety of place-names: Lugo in Russia; Lugansk in Ukraine; Lugoj in Romania; Lugo in Spain; several called Lugudunum (the city of Lugus) in France, of which the most famous is Lyons; Leiden in Holland; Louvain in Belgium; and Lugano in Switzerland. In the British Isles there are Loudon and the Lothians in Scotland, and in England, Louth, Carlisle (Luguvallum), Luton and possibly even London. Ireland particularly has many place-names associated with Lugus, including County Louth (anciently Lughbhaidh).

What do we know about the name Lugus? The root suggests light as in the Latin, *lux*, but *lu* (loosely Celtic) also means small in stature. Other loose Celtic derivations include *lugios* meaning lightning, and *lougos*,

A Latin inscription to the god Lugus from Lugo in Galician Spain

raven, but most tellingly *lugos* is a deception or an oath (as made in a trading contract). The Celtic Lugus or Lugh – as he is known in Ireland – is known as *samildanach*, 'skilled in all the arts'; in Wales, he is Lleu 'of the skilled hand', a god associated with a multitude of skills and abilities. Most probably a form of 'catch-all' deity, through punning, his name meant many things at once, but central would be the links to light, trade and the deception of a successful trickster figure.

Lugus as the Roman Mercury

In his account of his campaigns to conquer the Gauls (roughly across modern-day France), Julius Caesar declared that their most important god was Mercury and 'that there are numerous images of him; they declare him the inventor of all arts, the guide for any road or journey, and they deem him to have the greatest influence for all money-making and traffic'. Caesar had clearly described Lugus, however, and was seeking to substitute the native god with a Roman god who best approximated the role, so as to integrate Roman custom with the newly-conquered Gauls. The Roman god most associated with trade and commerce and many other skills – although not very prestigious back in Rome – in conquered Gaul, Mercury started to become very important.

There was a long tradition in Gaul of celebrating the start of the harvest in what is now early August by having feasts and games, and these were centred on the city of Lugudunum, modern-day Lyons. When the emperor Augustus finally completed the conquest of Gaul around 12 BCE, he was confronted with the celebrations in Lugudunum and the games of Lugus as a major festival. In order to quell this source of native nationalism and minimise the possibility of revolt, Augustus renamed Lyons after himself and rededicated the games as the Augustine Games, erecting a special altar for the occasion. Although this kind of assimilation of native culture into Roman culture was common policy throughout Roman conquest, it does appear that the quashing of the Lugus cult was a high priority.

Part of the enduring celebrations at the beginning of the harvest was for all the people to ascend a local hill or mountain in a great assembly, at which there were feasts and games. So, many of the key hilltops in Gaul, some of them strategically important, were associated with the god Lugus. The Romans therefore took over the hilltops where assemblies took place and built shrines and commissioned new statues to a Lugus substitution, their own god Mercury.

After the Roman Empire was washed away in the tide of new peoples and cultures taking over Europe in the fourth and fifth centuries CE, Christianity gradually became the dominant religion of the European region. Christian Bishops were confronted by native peoples still celebrating harvest assemblies at the tops of mountains and shrines, and viewed statues of the Roman pagan god Mercury and the distant memory of Lugus as unacceptable. So a substitute Christian saint with many of the characteristics of Lugus was introduced to the shrines and later churches on the high hills.

This saint was of course St Michael, the leader of the Archangels and the heavenly warrior, who, with his flaming sword, does battle with Satan in the form of a dragon. This tradition of placing churches dedicated to St Michael on high places in order to tame the dragon of pagan energies is well-known in France and England at sites like Mont Saint Michel in Brittany, St Michael's Mount in Cornwall and St Michael's Chapel on the top of Glastonbury Tor in Somerset. So we can see that the enduring influence of Lugus was translated by the Romans into their God, Mercury, and then by Christianity into their dragon-slaying saint, Michael. If we bring this tradition more down to earth and into a human saintly form, we

St Michael, the warrior archangel with flaming sword, became the Christian form of Lugus

St Michael's Mount in Cornwall

can identify St George as another important saint who successfully vanquishes the pagan dragon which threatens the peace and sovereignty of the country, a legend found in many European countries.

In order to get the clearest understanding of the Lugus cult and its relationship with the beginning of the harvest, however, we have to cross the Irish Sea. Ireland was never conquered by the Romans and so Irish traditions about Lugus, although Christianised, have remained remarkably intact. Research in the 1950s in rural Ireland tracing the remaining traditions of Lugh, as he is known in Celtic tradition, revealed a rich seam of Irish life.

The Croagh Patrick pilgrimage route with a statue of the Saint and the mountain behind

Lugh in the Irish Tradition

For hundreds of years, Irish people have been making an annual pilgrimage up the stony path to the summit of Croagh Patrick, St Patrick's Mountain, close to the beginning of August. Held to be the place where St Patrick banished the pagan demons from controlling the high ground, this Christianised ritual came out of a much earlier tradition whereby a powerful earth god known as Crom Dubh, the dark or stooped one (stooped, because of carrying the new harvest on his back), was overcome by the warrior god Lugh so that Lugh came to hold the secret of agriculture for the Irish people. Croagh Patrick was also known as Aigle, or the place of assembly, and there were many such high places all over the Irish countryside traditionally honoured with assemblies and feasting at the time of the beginning of the harvest. In Ireland, this key annual festival linking the harvest God Lugh with assemblies and games was known simply as Lughnasa. Pre-Christian in origin, Lughnasa was taken over by the Church and became associated with saints such as St Anne (festival day July 26th) and St James (July 25th).

How did Lughnasa come to be such a key festival in the agricultural calendar of Irish life? To find out, we have to visit Irish legend and myth. Ireland was traditionally populated by waves of foreign invaders including the Tuatha De Danaan – the people of the goddess Dana – and the most recent invaders and current occupants, the Gaels. The earliest inhabitants, however, were the Fomorians, strange unworldly beings not very attractive to look at and sometimes depicted with only one leg. They were magicians and held the secrets of the land, in particular the secret of agriculture. Their King, a one-eyed monster called Balor, fell into conflict with Nuada, the newly-arrived King of the Tuatha de Danaan.

Balor had been told in a prophecy by a druidess that one day his grandson would kill him in battle. Consequently he confined his beautiful daughter, Eithne, to a high tower, so that she would never meet any man. However, in the legend, Cian, a Tuatha de Danaan disguised as a woman, gains access to Eithne and her handmaidens and spends a night with her. Although he escapes, he is tracked down and later killed by Balor. Meanwhile, Eithne has become pregnant and gives birth to three infant boys. All are named Lugh, but they are forcibly taken from Eithne by Balor's servant, wrapped in a blanket and carried down to the sea to be drowned. However, one of the Lugh infants falls from the blanket unnoticed, escapes drowning, is rescued and smuggled back to the mainland of Ireland and given to Cian's brother, the smith god, Goban, to be brought up far away on the Isle of Man. There, the young boy Lugh is fostered by Tailtiu, another goddess who has learned the secret of

The young warrior Lugh with sling and golden spear

agriculture. Goban brings up the boy as a young prince who learns many crafts and skills but especially smithing, the game of chess and the military skills of a warrior.

As a mature young man, Lugh returns to Ireland to seek service at Tara where reigns Nuada, the High King of the Tuatha de Danaan. Impressed by his many talents, which surpass everyone else in the court, Nuada invites Lugh to use his smithing skills to create magical new weapons with which to overcome King Balor and the Fomorians. The resultant battle of Mag Tured is one of the epic turning-points in Irish mythical history. In the battle, King Nuada is killed by Balor, but Lugh confronts his grand-father and the prophecy is realised as Lugh slays Balor by using his magical flaming spear to drive Balor's one eye through to the back of his head. He then confronts another Fomorian, Bres the Beautiful, only sparing his life in exchange for the secret of agriculture. Out of this conflict Lugh secures the throne, brings peace to the country and reigns for forty years.

In this epic story, we can see how Lugh uses his many skills to assume kingship, gain the secret of agriculture from the Fomorian magicians and protect the sovereignty of the land of Ireland for the Tuatha de Danaan. But there is a further twist to the story. Lugh is summoned to the bed of his dying foster-mother, Tailtiu, who has exhausted herself to the point of death by clearing the forests from the plain of Ireland and so making the land available for agriculture, a secret that only she holds. The time is August, the beginning of the harvest; the place, modern Teltown in County Meath. As she dies, she exhorts her stepson, Lugh, to remember and celebrate her sacrifice forever by holding a great assembly at Teltown each August. So is born the annual beginning of harvest festival, the assembly of Lugh, or Lughnasa.

Traditionally, Lughnasa takes place over a week or ten days around the end of July and the beginning of August and involves not only a great assembly of the whole community where judicial and other problems can be worked out, but also a great festival of arts and crafts, with competitions of fighting prowess and games such as horse-racing. It is also the time of the beginning of the harvest when all the people pray for clement weather and a good rich harvest over the coming weeks of August and September. From that point, the festival gradually emerges from its mythical and legendary beginnings into the history of Ireland and is still celebrated today in Christianised form in places throughout the Irish countryside.

The Irish myth of Lugh is the fullest account that has come down to us in history, but there is no reason to believe that the story of Lugh or Lugus overcoming the primeval 'owner' god of the land, wresting from him and gifting the common people with the secret of agriculture, then assuming the kingship and so guarding the sovereignty of the land, was not present as a basic myth all across Europe.

The Lughnasa games at Lough Owel in Co. Westmeath. From a print of 1837.

The legend of Lugh is present in Wales where Lleu Llaw Gyffes, Llew of the Skilled Hand, eventually overcomes his adversary Gronw with a magical spear thrust and gains the Welsh kingdom for himself. Llew then becomes the root of the Welsh royal dynasty of Llewellyn. In England, there are stories of the great August Festival of Morvah in Cornwall and the overcoming of a giant by a Lugh figure called Jack the Tinkard. And in the county of Wiltshire there is a tradition of a great cattle fair and games being held on St Anne's Hill, on July 26th every year from medieval times until it was eventually abandoned in 1939. There are probably other English places where Lughnasa festivals were traditionally held but these have been lost in the overlay of the Saxon-introduced Christian feast of the start of the Harvest, Lammas tide, where Lammas is the English for the Saxon *loaf-mass*, the first bread made from the new harvest grain.

Lugh and the Securing of London

Although England has few direct references to Lugh legends to rival Ireland and Wales, there is one Welsh legend from the ancient book of the Mabonogion which directly involves Lugh and the securing of the sovereignty of England and its capital city London. In this tale, the King of England is Lud, whom Celtic authorities acknowledge as the same as King Nudd or Nuada of the Irish legend, a name linked to the Romano-British temple of Nodens in Gloucestershire. King Lud becomes famous for

*Ludgate in the
17th century*

founding a sacred temple near St Paul's Cathedral and the gate to the city of London known as Ludgate on Ludgate Hill. Some people see the root of the ancient name for London as deriving from Lud's name, so this king is centrally tied up with the foundation and sovereignty of London as the capital city of England.

King Lud has a brother Llewelys, who has become the King of France and who is recognised as the wise and clever one. After a time of successful development of the city walls and many years of peace in London, King Lud is beset with three plagues – or national oppressions – which paralyse his role as king. First the court is infiltrated by a race of demons, the Coranians, who can hear everything that everyone thinks, making privacy and discrete rulership impossible. Then each May Day Eve, a huge scream is heard over the whole land, causing wives to abort their babies and men to cower at home, too fearful to be warriors in the king's army. Finally, at the Court's annual feast at the end of harvest, King Lud and all his courtiers fall asleep, and when they awaken they discover that all the food of the feast and harvest grain stored in the king's barns has been stolen and carried off by a huge giant.

King Lud receives no help for these problems from his fearful courtiers but manages to seek the help from his clever brother Llewelys, or Lugh as we would recognise him. Lugh, true to his role as master of all skills, gives advice on how to deal with each of the plagues. A poison can be prepared and put in the drinks of the Coranians, who when invited to a special feast all duly perish, enabling King Lud to regain privacy and royal authority. The scream on May Day Eve is due to two huge dragons fighting in the air. When exhausted from their conflict, they are enticed to fall into a pit filled with alcoholic mead specially prepared near Oxford (at the geographical centre of the land), where, after drinking the mead, they fall asleep. It is then easy to despatch them, entomb them in a stone coffin and bury them at Snowdonia in Wales, from where they will cause no further interference. So Lud regains the warriors for his army and the women of the land are again secure in their homes.

Finally, King Lugh advises his brother to stay awake in the court's harvest feast by splashing cold water over his head. By so doing he sees the giant (a definite Fomorian echo here!) stealing the food and making off with the harvest grain from the barns. King Lud runs after the giant, confronts him in combat, and the harvest thief is so shocked by the King's bravery that he offers to serve him thereafter. So by following the wise advice of his brother King Lugh of France, King Lud of London regains his authority as King of England. You will note how Lugh has again carried out his role as keeper of sacred kingship, guardian of the sovereignty of the land and saviour of the harvest bounty, so essential for survival of the nation as a whole. This legendary story tells us that the city of London, probably named after King Lud, only owes its peaceful existence and subsequent successful history to the many-talented harvest god, Lugh.

However, if London owes its stability, prosperity and success as a great city to the intervention and wise counsel of the great god Lugh, how does his influence come to bear on the Olympic Games in 2012?

The Olympic Games as a Global Lughnasa

The festival of Lugh, Lughnasa, is traditionally held over July and August, most usually from July 27th to August 12th. These are the exact days of the Olympic Games Festival in London in 2012! In addition, the ancient Olympic Games, founded at Olympia in 667 BCE, carry a similar myth to Lughnasa Games in Europe. The Greek Olympics were also founded as funerary games to remember fallen warriors and great heroes, and tended to last for about two weeks around the end of July into early August. The ancient Games finished in 337 CE and it was not until 1896 that the modern Olympic Games were revived with the first festival of sport at Athens. By the time the fourth set of Games were held in London in 1908, the timing of the Games had more or less settled into approximately the last weeks of July into early August. So over the centuries we can see a fascinating drawing-together of two traditions of festive games, the Lughnasa Games and the Olympic Games. Both are totally independent in their origins and traditions, but here in England, based in the city of London in July 2012, the two traditions come together and completely fuse in a Lughnasa Olympic Festival!

The St Michael or Lugh Alignment is oriented to an August 1st Lughnasa sunrise

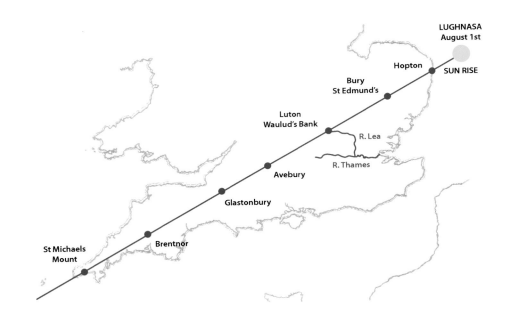

However, the influence of Lugh actually goes right to the centre of the Games at their main site at the Olympic Park in Stratford near Hackney, East London. Running across southern England from St Michael's Mount in Cornwall to Hopton on the Norfolk coast is a remarkable alignment known as the St Michael Line, first fully described by the late John Michell in the 1970s. This straight alignment passes through many high places and on the tops of these hills are churches dedicated to St Michael. Before Christianity, however, these places would be associated with Lugh. Sensitive dowsers have surveyed this alignment and identified a pair of intertwining masculine and feminine energies, which have been called the Michael and Mary currents. While academic archaeology is understandably silent or dismissive about such a mythic reality, the alignment is all the more fascinating in that it exactly faces sunrise in early May at the festival of Beltane and also in early August, at the festival of Lughnasa. The alignment, which we might rename the Lugh-Brigid line (Brigid being arguably the most celebrated indigenous goddess contemporary with Lugh), passes from St Michael's Mount through many Michael/Lugh sites across England, including Glastonbury and Avebury, as if there were a current of energy from Lugh's flaming spear crossing the land.

When the straight alignment and curving Michael/Lugh current crosses south Bedfordshire, they both pass through a suburb of the city of Luton. Luton, for some, is simply the town of Lugh, a foundation with its own mythic origins. Here in the suburbs there is a remarkable five-thousand-year-old Neolithic henge monument some seventeen acres in size, known as Waulud's Camp or Lygeanburgh – further reminders of Lugh. In the area of the henge are five sacred springs which combine together to form the start of the River Lugh, the river of modern Luton. However, when the Saxons came to England the River Lugh became the River Lea (lea is Saxon for meadow or field). Perhaps we can imagine the sacred springs of Waulud, sitting on Lugh's great alignment, tapping off some of the energy of Lugh's mythical spear and carrying it downstream. We follow the River Lea eastwards across the north of modern London and then southwards down the Lea Valley until the river divides up and embraces the whole of the Olympic Park at Stratford, thus ensuring that the entire Olympic area is imbued with the energy of Lugh.

The connection with Lugh does not simply involve the energies of the river, but also the land itself. Part of the Olympic Park is identified as Lammas Lands, that is, special land with ancient rights of grazing for commoners or local citizens. The period of grazing rights is from August 1st to March 25th, which is from Lammas-tide or Lughnasa to Lady Day or the commencement of the old calendar's New Year. During the nine-

*Waulud's Bank,
source of Lugh's river,
the River Lea,
at Luton*

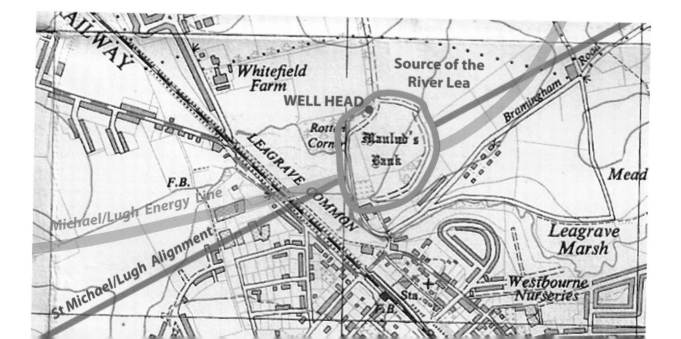

teenth century, the Lammas Lands were reduced by the city of London and developed into reservoirs and railway lines. Each time this happened and the citizens were offered compensation for losing their grazing rights, they insisted that part of the land be kept open for recreation. This tradition culminated in 1971 when almost all the remaining Lammas Lands were developed into football pitches and other sporting venues, making the Lea Valley famous for its recreational facilities. It is almost as if the Lugh energy and its mythic spirit of recreation and games were playing a part in shaping Lugh's Valley as a centre of sport and healthy competition for the city of London, many years before the area became identified as the site of London's Olympic bid.

Above all, Lugh is associated with grain and the fruits of the harvest. On the rivers of the Lower Lea Valley, exactly where the Olympic Park is now situated, were a number of great corn mills which used the tidal stream to power their grinding mechanism. The flour was then baked locally in adjacent Bow so that this East End suburb became known as the bakery of London. What could be more appropriate than the harvest god once again ensuring that the harvest is available for the people of the land?

In this remarkable example of living myth, we can see how the energy of the artful god Lugh contributes to the creation of the 2012 Olympic Games: he has fixed the time, July 27th to August 12th, and the place, the newly developed Olympic Park at Stratford City in the Lower Lea Valley. Surely this trickster god is also fixing the wider 'harvest' for London and all the nations of the world, with the first celebration of the Olympic Global Lughnasa.

*The Clock Mill, one of
the Bow tidal mills on
Lugh's river,
the River Lea,
once ground corn to
provide bread
for London*

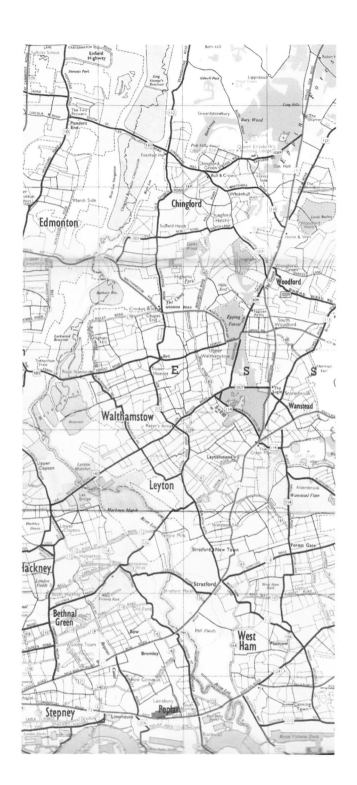

The Lower Lea Valley

LUGH'S RIVER: THE RIVER LEA

Louise Coe

London chose the Lea Valley as the site for the Olympic Games and this has drawn vast numbers of people to the area, which until recently was way off the beaten track for tourists seeking to discover the capital. Lying to the east of the City of London, far beyond its original boundaries, the area has a fascinating history, mainly due to the presence of the River Lea which flows through and round the Olympic Park on its way down to the Thames.

The Lea is a gentle river and until the nineteenth century the Lower Lea Valley was a tranquil meadowland. In the twelfth century, religious houses chose to establish themselves by the rich pastures. A Cistercian monastery, Langthorne Abbey, was established on the eastern banks of the Lea and it is on the former abbey lands that the Olympic Park now stands. Once the fifth largest abbey in England, owning extensive lands and using the river-water to power its mills, Langthorne came to be a popular retreat for royalty and the nobility until the Dissolution in 1539 and its subsequent destruction. Nearby at Bromley by Bow on the Lea, the Priory of St Leonard's was founded as a nunnery, offering a place of quiet contemplation.

The watery marshlands were cultivated on a small scale with a mixture of farming, market gardening and river fishing. Londoners would travel east to spend pleasant days out among the meadows and orchards around Bow and Hackney. In 1664, Samuel Pepys wrote in his diary, '…and thence after dinner by coach with my wife only to take the ayre, it being very warm and pleasant, to Bowe and Old Ford, and thence to Hackney. There 'light and play at shuffle-board, eat cream and good cherries; and so with good refreshment home.…'

The Lea provided water to power eight grain mills that were dotted along its banks. To the north, the Order of Knights Templar owned corn mills which are remembered in the coat of arms of Hackney, which

An original stone from Langthorne Abbey, also known as West Ham Abbey, now in All Saints Church, West Ham

incorporates the insignia of the Templar Cross. Despite the presence of these corn mills, for many years the extremely marshy conditions of the valley hampered any more extensive development.

Mile End marks where the East End begins, stretching along the Bow Road to the Lea Valley. Exactly one mile from the City of London, Mile End is a marker point for travellers into and out of the city. The East End served London in all kinds of important ways. For example, the city's bakers were based here, producing bread each day for delivery along the road into the city and as far away as Westminster. Similarly Tower Hamlets, just by the city's eastern boundary, gets its name because the Tower of London guards lived there.

As the city experienced the shift to an industrialised base of production, with growth in scale and speed, London could no longer sustain itself. Everything that the people did not want within the city was transferred to the East End. This burgeoning area was chosen for the siting of noxious industries, such as leather tanneries and slaughter houses. Fortunately for the established City of London and the more salubrious 'West End', the predominant winds were from the west and so polite society was spared the worst of the aerial pollution. A planning law passed in 1844 banned any industrial development within fifty yards of a domestic dwelling, whereupon all such sites were built to the east. The people living here

Bow locks near Bromley-by-Bow close to where the Lea joins the Thames

suffered enormously and were effectively the underbelly of the great story of London's success. The East End was called the city of the damned or outcast London, and became a place where industrialised London development sited beyond the jurisdiction of effective planning laws or the right to complaint caused the Lea to become so polluted that it was said that the waters ran purple.

The district where the Thames and the River Lea meet stands as the gateway to London. Here ships and boats arrive and depart, connecting London with the world. In his novel, 'Heart of Darkness', Joseph Conrad describes fortune-seekers leaving from the East End to build the Empire.

> 'They had sailed from Deptford, from Greenwich, from Erith — the adventurers and the settlers; kings' ships and the ships of men on 'Change; captains, admirals, the dark "interlopers" of the Eastern trade, and the commissioned "generals" of East India fleets. Hunters for gold or pursuers of fame, they all had gone out on that stream, bearing the sword, and often the torch, messengers of the might within the land, bearers of a spark from the sacred fire. What greatness had not floated on the ebb of that river into the mystery of an unknown earth!...
> The dreams of men, the seed of commonwealths, the germs of empires.'

Throughout the East End, the huge numbers of people chasing work meant low wages and poor conditions. This picture was not a new one for the area. Since Tudor times, ships' crews had landed here and been paid off for the voyage, the crew dispersing to seaman's colonies and poor lodging houses in the East End. It is now acknowledged that London's general expansion, and the West India Docks in particular, were built upon the proceeds of the Atlantic slave trade. Conditions for all types of workers were very poor. The East End housed the majority of the dock workers who were terribly exploited by unregulated labour laws and greedy employers.

A description from 1889 paints a picture of deprivation: 'The poor fellows are miserably clad, scarcely with a boot on their foot, in a most miserable state.... These are men who come to work in our docks who come on without having a bit of food in their stomachs, perhaps since the previous day; they have worked for an hour and have earned 5d. [about 2p]; their hunger will not allow them to continue: they take the 5d. in order that they may get food, perhaps the first food they have had for twenty-four hours.'

The East End has traditionally absorbed waves of immigrants, each of which has added a new dimension to the culture and history of the area. These included French Protestant Huguenots in the seventeenth century, the Irish in the eighteenth century, Ashkenazi Jews fleeing European pogroms towards the end of the nineteenth century and the Bangladeshi community settling in the East End since the 1960s. Immigrant communities tended to settle here because they came by boat along the Thames, landed by the Lea and made a start on their new lives right where they landed.

The Energy of Lugh

The River Lea actually rises seventy miles north of the docklands in Luton, where five springs converge. Here beside the springs are the remains of Waulud's Bank, a Neolithic site older than Stonehenge. According to legend, the Celtic god Lugh drank from the springs and gave them their power. The river, rising in Luton or Lughston, is named after the ancient pre-Roman god, Lugh, sometimes known as the Sun God of Light.

As we delve into the history of the Lea, it is fascinating to find the fiery energies of Lugh playing out along the river. Legends tell of Lugh's exploits and how his successes arise through intelligence and insight rather than brute force. A trickster and experimenter, he is called the Shining One, Lugh of the Long Hand, and He Who is Skilled in All the Arts. And it would appear that his many gifts remain at the disposal of those who trouble to seek him out, for his multifarious talents seem to find powerful echoes along the banks of his river.

A string of inventions have led some people to claim that the twentieth century was born in the Lea Valley. Among industry firsts are the fermentation of grains at Three Mill Island to produce acetone, the

The boating lake created by the River Lea at Wardown Park, Luton

invention of the diode flame which led directly to the wireless and ushered in the electronic age, and the invention of plastics and petrol. At the mouth of the Lea, Michael Faraday, who virtually invented electricity, worked to develop optics in London's only lighthouse. These are just a few examples; astonishingly, along the entirety of the River Lea over one hundred industrial inventions were developed. It is easy to see how the spirit of this river generates ground-breaking innovative concepts that go on from here to be taken up all round the world.

Alongside the scientific and industrial inventions that have gone on to transform our world are innovative social ideas, fiery uprisings and new radical thinking. The Lea Valley was for years the industrial centre of London and the unregulated factories and docks and cramped over-crowded workshops brought horrendous suffering to the people. In 1888, the match girls of Bryant and May, a matchstick- making factory in Bow, went on strike for better working conditions, the first ever strike in England by an unskilled female workforce. This, combined with the many strikes and organised industrial protests in the same era, made the East

Bow Creek Lighthouse used by Michael Faraday to develop optical refinements

Bryant and May's advert of 1897 reflecting improved working conditions following the women's strike of 1888

End a key element in the foundation of modern socialist and trade union organisations, as well as being a centre of the Suffragette movement demanding voting rights for women. Towards the end of the nineteenth century, a new wave of radicalism came to the East End, arriving with Jewish émigrés fleeing Eastern European persecution, and Russian and German radicals avoiding arrest.

The Lea Valley is an area that has seen the greatest depths of human misery, which caused passionately-driven workers' uprisings that led to reforms and social change. People from many cultures have settled here over the centuries. It is true to say that the East End community has significantly helped shape the new multi-cultural Britain that we now see not only as a central part of London culture but also emerging more widely around the country. The extraordinarily inventive minds that have been at work developing new ways to do things in the Lea Valley are a pronounced theme. Are these signs that the energy of Lugh is still at work in the area?

With the Olympic bid won on a sustainability ticket, we have witnessed a vast site development and building programme proceeding at breakneck speed, with sustainable design at the forefront. As ever, the area by-passed the stricter planning laws applied elsewhere, but this enabled the construction of some really spectacular architectural designs. With the huge level of innovation that is the history of the Lea River, it will be interesting to watch for new concepts emerging for the twenty-first century. Hopefully they will be adopted in a more balanced way than the take-up of petrol or plastic, which alongside their many benefits have been such an environmental scourge in our world.

The Olympic site is built upon the Lea, and it has been encouraging to see the cleansing of the ground-waters of the Lea as part of the site preparation. The river winds through and round the Olympic Park in a remarkable way, and the landscaping has been carried out as if to ensure that no part is not to feel the influence of Lugh's sacred water. These are the Bow Back Rivers, a complex of waterways created from the Lea to power the old industrial mills. The site is designed to interact with the waters of this network of rivers: the River Lea, Three Mills River, the

Prescott Channel, the Channelsea River, City Mill River and Waterworks River. The organisers of the Olympic Games have made a commitment to leave a lasting legacy in the area of the Lower Lea Valley, but it remains to be seen how that will play out.

The city of London in all its wonderful complexity can be seen as the gift of its rivers. Both the Thames and the Lea have fostered the city's great history. The Thames has enabled the establishment of enduring security, the authority of government and the success of commerce, finance and international trade, whilst the Lea has been a source of innovation and social reform, the great engine-room and powerhouse of a successful trading nation, indeed perhaps the ultimate guarantor of national sovereignty.

When we consider our natural reverence for water as the sacred source of all wisdom, and contemplate the energies and contributions of Isis, Sophia, St Mary and Lugh, it is shocking to realise just what it means to bury a river under concrete and modern development. The revitalisation of the River Lea as it flows through the Olympic Park could become a symbol of a new attitude of social energy and responsibility toward our rivers. When the world is watching the Olympics, perhaps the seeds of new thought may once again emerge from the Lea, join with the Thames, flow into the ocean and spread around the world.

The Olympic Stadium here under construction in 2009, is surrounded by the Bow Back Rivers which have now been extensively cleaned up and attractively landscaped

Satellite observation of
Amazon Rainforest
deforestation in the
Brazilian State of
Mato Grosso

AFTERWORD

Anthony Thorley

As the wheel of history slowly turns and we slide deeper into the twenty-first century, there is little doubt that profound changes are in the air for the entire global family. Through the early years of the first decade of the new century, the reality of those changes has nosed closer and closer into universal experience. We have all witnessed profound acts of terrorism in our own homelands, resulting in tightened home security and enduring wars in distant countries. We have all seen one massive tsunami affecting the seaboard of an entire ocean and more recently another, creating a nuclear emergency for an entire nation. Other effects of devastating earthquakes and unpredicted volcanic activity have caused profound social displacement of and disruption to whole communities and cultures. We read every day of relentless drought and raging bush fires, of worsening famine, of huge rainfalls and flash floods in the most unexpected places. Even those of us who have escaped direct tragedy and loss can share stories of weird weather: spring-times advanced by almost a month, summer flowers in November and the constant controversy about the human role in climate change.

Conversely, in the midst of all these extraordinary natural processes our global culture proceeds apace into the deepest complexities of an information age. We are united as never before by information technology, the universality of the world wide web and the extraordinary ubiquity of the mobile phone. With much of this change exploding into our culture within the last fifteen years, we now have a level of social connectedness and interaction which is entirely unprecedented in our known history. Nearly two hundred years ago, news of Napoleon's death on St Helena took over three months to reach the crowned heads of Europe. Today, any news, however significantly good or bad, encircles the entire world in minutes so that any form of cultural social isolation becomes rarer by the day.

Access to shared information brings comparisons and contrasts between countries with differing economic systems and potentials, causing great strains and cracks within those nations with repressive and controlling regimes, leading to revolution and internal conflict. However, and perhaps not unsurprisingly, a significant and central theme of this great social leavening, both politically and economically, is that it is imbued with an underlying sense of optimism. At the levels of economic opportunity, provision of basic living standards, health care, the chance for international travel without restriction, and improving freedom and human rights, despite glaring exceptions to these basic features of human existence and the important contribution of those who remain deeply critical of the way in which we husband our planet, there is a real sense that the world is a better place for most of us than it was even fifty years ago.

Such an unprecedented and unique period of rapid change in our global history seems to have been anticipated and even predicted by traditions from many cultures. A remarkable number of them, including the Mayan Long Count calendar which identifies 2012 as a pivotal year, have indicated that our present time-period is a culmination of a 26000-year process. Every year from around 1996 through to 2026, the rising midwinter sun has been positioned approximately in the centre of our galaxy. For the ancients, this was a sign that after 26000 years the sun had finally returned to the position of its own place of birth, and with this symbolic solar rebirth, mankind would enter a new era. In the years after 2026, the precessing sun will drift beyond this alignment and begin a new journey of 26000 years around the great ages of the zodiac, with mankind's new way of being settling into what will be hopefully an improved place.

It is also notable that nestling within this thirty year time-span we have the unique experience of a double transit of Venus, first on June 8th 2004 and then again on June 6th 2012 (which is intriguingly also the time of the Diamond Jubilee). Visible transits of the planet Venus across the face of the sun are rare events, only happening once in about every one hundred

The transit of the planet Venus across the face of the Sun, June 8th 2004

and twenty one years. They often occur in pairs, eight years apart, as it takes almost precisely eight years for Venus to return to its exact same position in the sky. The previous three eight-year pairs of Venus transits have all been associated with remarkable changes in universal consciousness, with an emphasis on exploration, communication and social revolution. Between 1631 and 1639, this was the birth of the Enlightenment and the scientific revolution; between 1761 and 1769, the industrial revolution in England and anticipation of the great political revolutions in America and France; and between 1874 and 1882, the great electrical revolution: invention of the telephone, the first transatlantic telephone cable and the application of the electric motor and light-bulb.

The Venus transits in 2004 and 2012 show the same pattern emerging again, this time with a strong emphasis on communication and revolution. There have been countless examples of new information technology in the last eight years, one of the most remarkable of which is the social network Facebook. Launched in 2004, eight years later Facebook has 845 million users, and indeed we could be said to be living in the

Facebook Age! And revolution is also strongly in the air as we witness the Arab Spring. The Venus transit experience always seems to produce extraordinarily creative processing moments for new ideas and far-reaching world change.

In 1999, I learned first-hand of another perception of the changes from two remarkable Chinese divination masters. In their thirties at the time, this young couple carry a family tradition of Yi Jing divination, personally advising Emperors and Presidents, which goes back into the thirteenth century and forward through many imperial dynasties to Chairman Mao himself. The two masters spoke only a little English and had never been outside China before, but for the first time felt called to share some of their tradition and wisdom with people in the West. At the end of three very busy days of consultations here in England with a variety of people (which intriguingly included a Government minister!), we all sat down for a final dinner together. One of the masters drew a Yi Jing trigram, Gen (mountain), on his paper napkin and through our excellent Chinese interpreter posed the question: 'According to our tradition, this trigram represents the time period between 2003 and 2024. What do you think it means?'

The Gen Trigram: 'Darkness is drawing to an end and brightness is coming. All things should have a new start'.

While I was completely mystified, my wife made a reasonable interpretation by suggesting that whilst heaven remained firm, the world below fell away. The master graciously acknowledged her bold suggestion as 'not bad', and explained that the trigram showed that it was as if, in 2003, mankind would enter a dark cave from which we would emerge in 2024, into a very different world. How that world might be in 2024, however, no one could say since it would depend on the choices we would make whilst in the cave, but apparently this time-period carried the potential to bring about the greatest change that might ever affect mankind. To me, this Chinese prophecy was all the more impressive since our Chinese friends had absolutely no knowledge of the Mayan tradition or any of the Western or other traditions and predictions which were emerging at the time.

So as we progress through the years around 2012, we are well and truly inside that cave of contemplation and choices, and as we are finding out, the lessons we have to learn are profoundly challenging. Since 2008, we have seen one of the traditional seven deadly sins, greed, drive us over the edge into financial collapse and a world recession from which we may not fully recover until the early 2020s. Additionally, we are in a chronic energy crisis: oil supplies are slowly dwindling; energy prices are spiralling upwards, threatening whole economies and lifestyles; and we are slow to curb our voracious consumption and embrace the fulsome use of sustainable energy sources that are free of pollution and technical disaster. Can we develop the collective commitment to surmount these difficulties?

In the preceding chapters, we have shown that the *genius loci* of London, the spirit of London as a sacred city, has been present ever since the city was established in ancient times, and how its spiritual heart has been nurtured by the Thames and its attendant rivers, and revitalised again and again by the myths, legends and history of its people. We have drawn attention to two particular occasions in living history when that spirit was consciously further strengthened and protected by man himself: in the development and ideals of the deeply symbolic pattern of Elizabethan theatres and the encryption of Sir Christopher Wren's geomantic master-plan in the pattern and design of his City churches.

And now, after centuries of nurturing and preparation, it is as if the essential spirit of London as a great city has reached out and in the year of 2012 called the world to come and experience the warmth of our welcome and the richness of our culture, and celebrate with us the Queen's Diamond Jubilee, a great restatement of the sovereignty of our land (surely Lugh would approve!); the Olympic Year Festival of the Arts (one thinks especially of the World Shakespeare Festival at The Globe theatre echoing the great pattern of Elizabethan theatres); and most significantly, the Olympic and Paralympic Games as a global Lughnasa. If the spirit of London can have its own dreamtime, dreaming these great festivals into reality, then surely 2012 can be seen pre-eminently as the year of the Olympic Dream, awakening mankind into a great new era.

All of these celebrations are inherently positive, offering hope, optimism and a deep-felt belief in the power of the human spirit to transcend the great difficulties of the world and achieve a new era of harmony and cooperation. Even when we feel surrounded by tribulation and sobering *realpolitik*, the festivals of 2012 – centred on the sacred city of London – can offer the world a taste of the positive and the promise of resolution. However, there should be no rose-tinted spectacles! We live in a practical world facing harsh realities, and although the pivotal year of 2012 can bring the world a sense of hope, it may be some years more – as reflected in the Chinese tradition – before we finally decide upon all our choices and find it is time to leave the cave and the shadows and walk out into the sunlight.

Gatekeeper Pilgrims walking out into the sunlight

ABOUT THE GATEKEEPER TRUST

The Gatekeeper Trust is a Registered Educational Charity founded in 1980 and devoted to personal and planetary healing through pilgrimage.

In particular, it seeks to rediscover the ancient art of pilgrimage as a way of journeying with an awareness of the sacred nature of our environment. It researches both ancient and modern knowledge about the landscape and shares it through an annual programme of journeys, workshops and conferences. As well as being nationally organised, the Trust has a number of active local groups and publishes an annual magazine.

Sacred Journeys

Shared journeys unite people and engender respect for different cultures, the land we live upon and the environment that sustains us. A journey is an adventure that can be both challenging and a joyful experience. Above all, we believe that the act of pilgrimage or a sacred journey can contribute to a more peaceful and healthy world.

In these busy times, we have almost forgotten how to walk on the Earth in a simple and sacred way with awareness. The Gatekeeper Trust seeks to recover this ability to be in tune with the landscape. We offer journeys and workshops where people can re-discover their connection with the Earth and with Spirit in a simple and loving way.

Each of us knows at least one place where we feel special – somewhere that makes us seem more alive, more in tune with the world, more truly ourselves. It is here that we connect with the spirit of place and find universal harmony.

As we care for places in the landscape, we find that places in ourselves become healed. Journeys through the outer landscape can create within us new frontiers of inner perspective; we discover new depths of potential in ourselves that may have lain hidden before; new gifts can be released in us.

The Earth herself has an abundance of simple gifts to be enjoyed. We invite you to discover them with us.

How does walking help the Earth?

With an understanding of how energies move through the Earth, it can be realised that just as acupressure can restore the healthy flow of vital energy in humans, so walking with conscious awareness can help Mother Earth. Today this way of caring for the Earth is mostly a lost knowledge. Yet, historically, pilgrimage formed a central core to society. In medieval times, for instance, pilgrimage routes were established all over Europe.

The Australian Aborigines still go on their 'walk-abouts', walking their 'song lines' very much in tune with the needs of their land. Walking in this way can enhance natural energies that flow through the Earth's crust, as can dance, song and prayer, all helping to bring healing and balance to the environment and to the planet as a whole.

The Gatekeeper Trust researches this landscape knowledge and shares it through an annual programme of sacred journeys, workshops, conferences and link-in events at both a local and national level.

As a small Educational Charity, we rely on the membership as our lifeblood. We are always grateful for any donations and help to enable us to continue this valuable work.

For further information about the Gatekeeper Trust including details of how to join, please contact the secretary of the Trust.
Email secretary@gatekeeper.org.uk or go to www.gatekeeper.org.uk

ACKNOWLEDGEMENT

The authors would like to thank the many friends, colleagues and wise members of the Gatekeeper Trust who have given support and assistance during the production of this book. In particular, we recognise the tireless work and dedication of Sarah Dawkins, an elder of the Gatekeeper Trust and for many years primary organiser of the Trust's Winter Conferences.

CONTRIBUTORS

Louise Coe has a particular interest in the rivers of Britain and their sacred nature. She practises Interior Alignment, which combines the art of Feng Shui and Space Clearing and leads groups in exploration of the eight solar Festivals of the year.
See www.inneralignment.co.uk

Peter Dawkins, a founder-member of the Gatekeeper Trust, is known particularly as a pioneer and leading teacher in the science of landscape temples (geo-cosmology) and their connection with mythology and the wisdom teachings.
See www.zoence.co.uk and www.peterdawkins.com

Chris Street has been working with the 'Visionary Landscape' since the early 1980s when a series of dreams and visions initiated his discovery of the Earthstars system around London. He is the author of several books and has been a member of the Order of Bards, Ovates and Druids for over twenty years.
See www.earthstars.co.uk

Anthony Thorley is a retired psychiatrist who has been researching landscape energies and traditions for over thirty years. He teaches Sacred Geography at University of Wales, Trinity St David, where he is studying for a PhD on the conceptual basis of landscape zodiacs as sacred space.
See www.earthskywalk.com and www.thealchemicaljourney.co.uk

This book was commissioned by the Gatekeeper Trust. The views presented here are strictly those of the authors and do not necessarily represent those of the Gatekeeper Trust or its members.

Ackroyd, Peter (2001) London: The Biography, Vintage, London.

Ackroyd, Peter (2008) Thames: Sacred River, Vintage, London.

Ashe, Geoffrey (1990) Mythology of the British Isles, Methuen, London.

Bachelard, Gaston (1994) Water and Dreams, Dallas Institute of Humanities and Culture, Dallas.

Barton, N J (1992) The Lost Rivers of London, Historical Publications Ltd., London.

Broadhurst, Paul and Robin Heath (2009) The Secret Land, Mythos, Launceston, Cornwall.

Broadhurst, Paul and Hamish Miller (1990) The Sun and the Serpent, Mythos, Launceston, Cornwall.

Caine, Mary (1978) The Glastonbury Zodiac, Kingston on Thames.

Dawkins, Peter (1998) Zoence: the Science of Life, Red Wheel/Weiser, New York.

Dawkins, Peter (2002) The Shakespeare Enigma, Polair Publishing, London.

Devereux, Paul (2010) Sacred Geography, Gaia, London.

Dreiseitl, Herbert (2009) Recent Waterscapes, Birkhauser GmbH, Boston.

French, Karen (2012) The Hidden Geometry of Life, Watkins Publishing, London.

Gilbert, Adrian (2002) London: a New Jerusalem, Bantam Press, London.

Gordon, E O (1913) Prehistoric London, its Mounds and Circles, Covenant Publishing, London.

HRH Prince of Wales, Tony Juniper and Ian Skelly (2010) Harmony, Blue Door, London.

Hancox, Joy (1997) The Byrom Collection, Jonathan Cape, London.

Hancox, Joy (2001) Kingdom for a Stage, Sutton Publishing, Stroud.

Heath, Robin and John Michell (2004) Measure of Albion, Bluestone Press, St Dogmael's.

Jardine, Lisa (2002) On a Grander Scale, Harper Collins, London.

Jenkins, John Major (2002) Galactic Alignment, Bear and Company, Rochester, Vermont.

MacNeill, Maire (1962) The Festival of Lughnasa, Oxford University Press, Oxford.

Matthews, John and Chesca Potter (1990) The Aquarian Guide to Legendary London, Aquarian Press, London.

Merz, Blanche (1988) Points of Cosmic Energy, C W Daniel and Co Ltd., London.

Michell, John (1975) The Earth Spirit, Thames and Hudson, London.

Michell, John (2012) How the World is Made, Thames and Hudson, London.

Pogacnik, Marco (2008) Sacred Geography, Lindisfarne Books, New York.

Schwenk, Theodore (1996) Sensitive Chaos, Rudolph Steiner Press, London.

Smith, Jill (1985) The Gypsy Switch, P V Cozens, Llaneli, Dyfed.

Smith, Jill (2000) The Callanish Dance, Capall Bann, Chieveley, Berkshire.

Starkey, David (2012) Royal River, Scala Publishers Ltd., London.

Stray, Geoff (2005) Beyond 2012, Catastrophe or Ecstasy, Vital Signs Publishing, London.

Street, C E (1990) Earthstars, Earthstars Publishing, London.

Street, Christopher (2010) London, City of Revelation, Earthstars Publishing, London.

Street, Christopher (2009) London's Camelot and the Secrets of the Grail, Earthstars Publishing, London.

Street, Christopher (2010) London's Ley Lines, Earthstars Publishing, London.

Thorp, Ian (2011) The Great Year: Understanding 2012 and Beyond, Archive Publishing, Wimborne, Dorset.

Thorley, Anthony (2012) Sir Christopher Wren's Secret London, Archive Publishing, Wimborne, Dorset.